BALKAN HOURS

BALKAN HOURS

Travels in the Other Europe

RICHARD BASSETT

JOHN MURRAY

First published in 1990
by John Murray (Publishers) Ltd
50 Albemarle Street, London, w1x 4bd

British Library Cataloguing in Publication Data
Bassett, Richard
Balkan hours: travels in the other Europe.
1. Eastern Europe. Description and travel
I. Title
914.7
ISBN 0–7195–4721–0

Printed in Great Britain by Butler and Tanner Ltd
Frome and London

CONTENTS

ILLUSTRATIONS

For Emma-Louise

INTRODUCTION

A few miles south of Vienna lie the woods of Baden. Here, along leafy paths, Beethoven and Schubert were accustomed to wander, seeking inspiration in hills whose pine trees are very different from the impenetrable hanging curtains of green familiar to most Alpine travellers. These trees are short, evergreen umbrellas swaying gently in the warm wind which is rarely absent from these parts. A few years ago, an old Austrian took me up one of those hills on a bright spring morning. If I closed my eyes, he told me, I would smell the Adriatic. I did as I was told and experienced that faint warmth which for a host of nineteenth-century Germans making their way over the Alps was the first hint of the south.

From here the crow flies not to Venice but Trieste, the Eastern Adriatic and the Balkans. This perspective is important. In Graz, a silver-haired man with whiskers wanted to talk to me about Bosnia, not Verona. Later, in Trieste, I encountered the first of a remarkable series of human survivors of an earlier order whose general air of aristocratic *sprezzatura* was in strange counterpoint to the prevailing atmosphere of communist corruption that had seized the peninsula. Thanks to a small talent on the French horn, I was usually able to earn my keep by 'blarstin', as my music master used to call it, at opera scores. There are shortages of many things the northern European traveller considers 'civilised' in the Balkans but opera houses are not one of them. Only once – in Ljubljana where the audition panel consisted of three percussionists and two octogenarian house porters – did this lead to full employment. Even then my inability to prevent myself from falling asleep while counting my rests in the final act of *La Bohème* often jeopardised this income.

The Opera was an early introduction to the chaos of Balkan intrigue which, combined with the passions which so often dominate artistic life, proved at times quite explosive. On one occasion, as a result of some minor dispute between the conductor of *Swan Lake*

1

and one of the more baroque girls in the *corps de ballet*, make-up was applied to blacken out most of the teeth of the dancers whose inane toothless grins, aimed towards the front row of visiting communist dignitaries, at the height of the drama drove their opponent to the brink of violent derangement.

Weekends, after the inevitable Friday schools' matinée performance of Prince Igor, were spent exploring. In forty-eight hours one could be remotely established near some great Orthodox monastery of the Serbs or consuming that fatal glass of rakir beneath the white limestone arches of Robert Adam's Spalatro. The Balkan Peninsular probably offers the most varied tapestry of conflicting religions, landscapes and races in Europe. Though everyone who travels the area will have his own view of what precisely the Balkans are, all must agree that as we approach the end of the century the 'other Europe', stretching east from Trieste down towards Istanbul, is still suspended in a web of conflicting loyalties and intrigues. Not surprisingly, by the time I had played the First Horn part of *La Bohème* for the twenty-fifth time, my interest in the Balkans had increased as my delight in Puccini waned. I had been in fact seduced by that combination of unrivalled architecture, spectacular scenery and bravado which, as these pages may show, are still the jewels of Balkan life.

1 TRIESTINE PRELUDE

'Wake up, stay up! The English fleet, *die Flotte*! It is war, young man, it is *KRIEG*!' The by no means unimpressive figure of the eighty-year-old Countess Blanka von Korvin-Giustiniani stood near my bed, a slightly trembling hand holding a cup of hot Turkish coffee.

It was more than a month since I had taken up residence in the Giustiniani household in a rundown late-eighteenth-century town flat in the heart of Trieste, a biscuit's throw away from the Adriatic. Blanka, friends had warned, was a 'little eccentric'. All those years in an Albanian prison had, they assured me, unhinged her mind, and then her past – at this point those who knew her shook their heads – yes, her past was extraordinary; a warning to everyone of the challenge and bitterness of life. Few had known so much luxury, fallen so low and now enjoyed such poverty.

But though the kitchen in the Via XXX Ottobre had clearly not been modernised since 1910, and while one by one the faded old bits of wooden furniture, pearl-inlay tables from Constantinople, Empire mirrors and *jugendstil* statues were sold to make ends meet, Blanka resolutely refused to economise on coffee. In her dark kitchen relieved only by her sombre oil paintings and the oriental patterns she painted on the walls as a frieze, the coffee was made each day. During the night, accompanied by the occasional pair of friendly cockroaches scuttling across the stone floor, she would sit in front of a foot-high flame of gas coming from a battered hob which at any moment threatened to blow the entire house to bits. Somehow, in defiance of all natural laws, the explosion never occurred, the flame was lowered and the coffee poured into a small cup and brought to my bed each morning at 8 a.m. Being young and of a generally lazy disposition, my initial reaction to this was to feign sleep. But that was rarely successful as Blanka invariably declaimed some implausible but arresting phrase forcing me to take the cup, a sip of whose flavour banished all weariness.

James Joyce, who taught at the old Berlitz School above the Ponte-Rosso market two streets away from XXX Ottobre, once implored a friend to visit him in Trieste with the words 'You will see sun.' Certainly few cities so far north offer so much light and so little rain both in winter and in summer. When the rain came accompanied by the Bora, that harsh north-easterly wind which lightly breakfasts in Fiume and lunches in Capodistria before fiercely dining in Trieste, it was soon followed by the bluest of blue skies. Sunny morning followed sunny morning relentlessly during the spring until by early May the long faded jade green blinds at XXX Ottobre were drawn tightly down from 11 o'clock onwards.

Outside, the proximity of two magnificent churches underlined Trieste's cosmopolitan past. Along one road rose the splendid neo-classical pile of San Antonio, the Contessa's favourite place of worship under whose coffered ceiling she would be found promptly each evening between five and six. Beyond here, across a small strip of water once filled with ships but now hardly meriting its name of Canale Grande, rose the blue-domed Serbian Orthodox church.

'We are constantly being undermined. *Unterminiert* by Slavs!' Blanka would solemnly intone over breakfast. Not that she meant the Serbs, a few old merchants descended from eighteenth-century families. For the Contessa and most of her class in the city, the threat was from the Slovenes, Slavs of the Julian Alps, tall, gifted, blond, but difficult people, the descendants of the last Slavs to penetrate the Eastern Alps.

After the war, the Allies had had to continue occupying Trieste as Slovenes from Marshal Tito's Jugoslavia fought with Italians for possession of the city and its Istrian hinterland. Eventually Istria, that beautiful peninsula whose rich soil produces the finest red wines and whose quarries supplied all of Palladio's white stone, became part of communist Jugoslavia, while Trieste, with a large Slovene minority (estimated at between 20,000 and 50,000) remained Italian. Ever since, relations between the two have been uneasy and offered me my first insight into that eternal dilemma of the Balkans, the struggle for national supremacy which so disfigures Balkan life.

Certainly few races are as different from each other, even in the Balkans, as the Slovenes and the Italians. While the Slovenes like all Slavs tend towards introspection, slow but methodical thinking, the Latins of Trieste appear sharper, livelier and above all quicker personalities. While you would wait for the Slovene waiter to attend to your order in a quiet dignified way in one café, in another, the Italian knew and noisily dispatched your wish almost before you had formulated it. There was no room, however, for a dispassionate appraisal of each race's merits by those who lived in Trieste. Not far from the Church of San Antonio runs the leafy promenade known as the Viale XX Settembre. Here, between the scores of café tables and the lines of acacia trees, young Italians used to gather, among them supporters of the MSI (Movimento Sociale Italiano) or neo-fascist movement. Occasionally they might parade up and down handing out leaflets to passers-by which demanded 'No Bilinguilismo' or to the introduction of the Slovene language into the city's official statutes. Slovenes complained bitterly at the Viale though I myself never saw, as they frequently alleged, any Slovene being abused on the avenue. In return, the Slovenes organised their own radio stations and marched along the great boulevard known as Cesare Battisti with grim-looking banners demanding an end to 'Italian ascendancy'.

The deadlock was and remains impossible to solve. Though the Italians who have enjoyed rivalry with the Croats and other Slavs are possibly more interested as a nation than anyone else in the concept of Central Europe, the Triestine Italians cannot look over their shoulders at the Slovene hinterland except in fear or distrust. Certainly the narrowmindedness of the Slovenes, who show many characteristics of their fellow Alpine-dwellers in Bavaria and Austria, is a powerful impediment to cordial relations. Men who flourished as bureaucrats under the Austrian Empire and women whose traditions rested on polite, domestic service are inevitably at a disadvantage in dealing with the more sophisticated Italians. Unhappy memories of Marshal Tito's forty-day occupation of the city at the end of the war have also left a bitter legacy of racial enmity.

The economic crisis of the city, once the great port of the Habsburgs but now barely more than a point on the Italian navy's map, does not assist the cause of racial harmony. But in the bars and boutiques a veritable power struggle is in train, with shops becoming the focus of takeover bids from one ethnic group or another. And the daily influx of Jugoslav shoppers meant until very recently that large sums of money were to be made from the visiting Serbs, Macedonians and Bosnians.

In contrast to the rather European-orientated Slovenes, the daily influx of Serbs and other southern Jugoslavs presented a picture of virtually oriental aspect. Debouching from crammed trains which had run into the opulent neo-Grecian Stazione Centrale, these crowds of pantalooned women with gold earrings accompanied by swarthy hillsmen dressed in long woollen jodphurs poured forth each day except Sunday and Monday, when the majority of shops were closed. Predictably, the more cultivated Slovenes loathed their southern kinsmen as much as the Italians did. But for many uneducated Italians, the difference between a Slovene and a Montenegrin was in any case an irrelevant point; they were all Slavs and therefore all either 'at your feet or at your throat'. The dirt and mess the thousands of Jugoslav shoppers left behind inevitably became another tool for Italian propagandists to beat the Slovenes with.

Blanka, being herself of Polish origin and therefore also a Slav, rose above this but long years in the German-speaking part of the Austrian Empire and a loathing for all things communist did not endear the Slovenes to her. 'Small-minded people. I'm not particularly *impressionated* with them,' was her inimitable verdict.

Born near Odessa in 1899, her father had served in the Austrian navy, rising to the rank of Captain and being attached to several embassies in turn as a naval attaché. His long, distinguished but slightly sad face rising from a dark blue naval uniform in a pre-1914 photograph dominated the chaotic mixture of Biedermeier chairs, desks and card tables which passed for Blanka's drawing-room or, in the parlance of Mitteleuropa, 'salon'. Much of the furniture, coming from a grander house, looked a little out of place in the modest flat.

In a tall glass cabinet which for some reason Blanka had insisted on painting a vivid scarlet, a small postcard bearing a finely drawn thumbnail sketch of a Russian wooden house was stuck into one of the frames. This was the house she had been born in, a small Chekovian villa not far from the Black Sea. In 1908, with her father posted to Constantinople, she had attended the German School with her three elder sisters: 'Four Korvins and four footmen to make sure we were not interfered with on the way in the Bazaar,' she would recall.

To say that the East was ever present with her is perhaps an exaggeration but in her patriarchal manner tempered by all the gentle flexible hospitality which I came to see as the hallmark of the Balkans, Blanka certainly possessed an almost impish playfulness which coexisted happily with a fervent devotion to the Catholic Church. This unusual combination of gravitas and a light touch made her a remarkable personality. At one moment, a voice ringing with aristocratic *sprezzatura* would dismissively remind one of duty and the overriding need to be punctual – *Bei uns waren die Leute erschossen wegen der Punktlichkeit'.** At other times devotion to the Almighty was tempered by a delight in telling slightly risqué jokes.

Religious devotion was to prove more than necessary in the years after the war when as an Italian in Albania† who did not manage to escape, she was imprisoned by partisans as a spy and tortured. That was a period of her life to which I never alluded, though occasionally Blanka would bring it up over breakfast as evidence of the life-giving properties of Catholicism. Only God had prevented her from going insane. Sometimes she spoke of visions.

Her experiences in Albania were all the more extraordinary as her life up to then had been a social whirl of parties and dinners. As the widow of an Italian Count all doors in Rome were open, and her eldest sister Christa had married into the Croatian aristocracy, so giving her an entrée to many of the salons of the neighbouring Kingdom of Jugoslavia, too. Along with snippets of life during the days of the Habsburg Empire, conversation often turned to the exciting years of the 1920s and the 1930s in Zagreb and Belgrade.

It is perhaps impossible for someone of the post-war generation to appreciate the tremendous respect all things British enjoyed in Europe before the war. 'First, the shoes,' Blanka explained, pointing out that no one's shoes ever shone brighter than those worn by the Englishmen she came across mostly in diplomatic circles. One was

---

*'With us people were shot for being late.'
†Albania was occupied by Mussolini, who annexed the country as a protectorate in 1939.

a consul in Africa called Smallbones. As an example of English discipline Blanka was fond of describing how, when on safari a Portuguese diplomat had an affair with Smallbones' wife, the Englishman was so depressed by his wife's distraction that he stormed into her lover's tent, prepared to grant his wife the chance to live with the man.

'Do you love my wife?' Smallbones asked.

'Of course not,' came the impudent reply.

'So what did he do?' Blanka asked rhetorically. Such a thing was clearly in her eyes grounds for violence, but Smallbones, though he felt angry beyond belief, only turned on his heels, grinding his nails into the palms of his hands. This degree of self-control in the face of such an unpardonable insult to his wife was unforgettable to Blanka, who after telling the story, embellished with vivid details, relapsed into the refrain: 'So great is your England.'

The most memorable Englishman for her was, however, the ill-fated Sir Nevile Henderson, the arch-appeaser and Britain's last ambassador to Nazi Germany. History has been far from kind to Henderson who, though clearly blind to the Nazi evil, does not appear to have deserved all the opprobrium hurled at him. If ever a man typified what Churchill referred to as England's 'carelessness, unwisdom and good nature', which almost undid the free world, Henderson was that man.

His good nature was evident in a sad postcard he sent to Blanka while sailing to South America after leaving his post as Minister in Belgrade. Over a faded sepia photograph of the Atlantic, a strong hand etched out in French the phrase: 'Nothing can help ease the pain that the memory of the events a year ago today brings.' The card was written one year after King Alexander of Jugoslavia, a close friend of Henderson's, was shot dead in Marseilles by Croat extremists. Another letter Blanka showed me was written a few days before war was officially declared. Headed on stiff white parchment with the words 'British Embassy, Berlin', it simply noted, 'This is madness. The Germans do not want war.'*

---

*One diplomat who remembers bringing the telegram of Britain's war declaration into Henderson's office recalled Sir Nevile's reaction as being 'a look of annoyance and the observation "To think we are going to war just to kick this dictator in the pants" '.

In his book, aptly named *Failure of a Mission*, Henderson comes over as an honourable man who was woefully misguided, refusing right up to the end to see that Hitler, if not necessarily the German people, was an evil which had to be destroyed. Even a year before he died of cancer (like his fellow arch-appeaser Chamberlain) Henderson could write that he liked and adored the German people. 'I feel myself very much at home among them and I find them less strangers than almost any other people.'

Blanka's explanation was that 'dear Nevile' had had a German governess as a child (in a house where according to the Contessa bowls of lettuce leaves were left in several rooms to prevent the children developing an appetite for sweets). But I could not help feeling, after hearing a description of a moonlight walk with Nevile along Lake Veldes in the Julian Alps (now Bled in Slovenia), that this pro-German sentiment may even have been fuelled by Blanka herself. The two were certainly, to judge from the correspondence, 'intimate' and on more than one occasion the weary diplomat in Berlin was said to have met 'discreetly' with the 'foreign countess' whose picture rested on his desk.

One of these occasions Blanka described in detail. Anxious to preserve the life of a German friend whom she feared would soon be arrested by the Nazis, she travelled to Berlin in the hope of enlisting Henderson's support. The meeting in early 1939 was brief and held in a room of the Hotel Adlon which was somehow linked through a passage to the Embassy Chancery next door so that British diplomats could leave without being seen by Gestapo guards. Perhaps Henderson knew he was approaching the end of his life. Perhaps he also knew that his policy was disintegrating in the face of Hitler's ever more outrageous demands. Blanka said he only expressed horror that she might come to harm in a city whose people knew she had anti-Nazi ideas. Her friend could in any event no longer be saved.

The effect of these reminiscences on a young mind can probably be gauged. Evening after evening the temptations of a night on the town were banished less by my lack of friends than by the promise of more instalments in the life and times of my *padrone* and a step back into European history. There are, I am assured, certain religious sects which believe the art of the raconteur to be a sacred gift bestowed only upon the few. Certainly I never met an intelligence so dazzling as to eclipse Blanka's in the sincerity and absorption of her anecdotes.

Nor was our conversation confined to the subjects of the past. Modern morals, theatre personalities, art, music, all were rigorously and openly discussed. From the local Italian aristocrat with a penchant for young boys – 'Such a story. Like the *Tod in Venedig*' – to the merits of marrying the woman you love – divine inspiration over rational calculation – the candles on the wall flickered and the level in the ubiquitous bottle of Baron Stock's brandy (distilled half a mile up the coast) fell lower and lower. It might be tempting to imagine that in Blanka the enquiring young mind had discovered something completely out of the ordinary. But though she was without doubt the most remarkable figure to pass through my life, she was not alone in expressing the values of an old order.

Trieste has a long and distinguished history of eccentric and gifted consuls. Richard Francis Burton, translator of *The Arabian Nights*, was one, Stendhal another. Ten years ago, beyond the Serbian Orthodox church high up in a neo-classical palazzo near the old Tergesteo arcade was the office of the French Consulate, then under the guidance of the eighty-four-year-old Baron Gottfried von Banfield. With a beaky profile and brilliant silver hair, his manners were impeccable. Since the British Foreign Office became a grey bureaucracy inhabited often by inarticulate and shabbily dressed men, it is difficult to recall the traditions of hospitality which once made diplomacy the great profession it was. Perhaps because Banfield was at heart first and foremost a soldier, he had a style all of his own. 'A little cognac, young man?' he ventured, pulling out from his mahogany desk a drawer deep enough to reveal two bottles of Stock brandy standing side by side. It was 11.30 in the morning. This was an early introduction into the Balkan habit of morning alcohol which muddies, sometimes blissfully, often dismally, so many minds on the peninsula.

As *The Times* obituary pointed out when he died in 1986, Banfield was a remarkable link with a lost chivalry. The son of an Irish officer in the Austrian navy, Banfield had been born in Castel Nuovo on the bay of that most formidably defensive harbour in the Adriatic, Cattaro (now Kotor), not many miles south of Dubrovnik. Trained first as a naval officer, Banfield swiftly switched to aircraft, becoming on the outbreak of war, a lieutenant in the hastily formed imperial naval air service. It was on a dazzling spring morning in 1916 that he found himself in Pola in command of a squadron as the aerodrome was attacked by Italian fighters. Despite express orders to remain where he was, Banfield took off by himself and saw the Italian fighters off, shooting down two and damaging a third.

Such reckless bravery had long been awarded the highest decoration for valour in the Habsburg Empire, the Maria Theresa Order, an honour that was won on more than one occasion by expressly disobeying orders. The decoration carried with it immediate promotion to the nobility with the title of Baron of the Austrian Empire. In Banfield's case this promotion was delivered along with the medal by no less a person than the Emperor Franz Josef. Banfield was therefore the only surviving recipient of an order dating back several hundred years, and one moreover whose roll-call would finally close when this man passed away. He was also given the soubriquet 'Eagle of Trieste' by the grateful inhabitants of the city.

Like Blanka, whom of course he knew well, the Baron had known both poverty and luxury, humiliation and glory. It is perhaps precisely because this generation learned the truth of Kipling's words that success and failure are both 'impostors' that they were able to carry such moral weight and appear so content with life. Like Blanka, Banfield had also spent some time in prison. When the Italians entered the city in 1918, the fabled 'Eagle of Trieste' who had accounted for so many Italian lives was, predictably, far from being a hero. The Italians threw him into prison, though he was later released and allowed to go to Vienna.

Banfield was happy to talk about these days and was also fascinated by England, whose nationality he had first enjoyed. England's problem though was – and here he leaned back in his chair and recalled his days as a penniless draughtsman in Newcastle in the 1920s – 'resistance to change'. 'Here in Italy we do things quicker because we have to, not as in England where I was told "My dear Geoffrey, we will do it this way because we have always done it this way".' At the time he told me this, when a Labour government was ruling Britain and strikes and inefficiency had become endemic in the country's life, Banfield's remarks appeared poignantly true. But even as we talked over the three-star brandy, political developments in London were taking place which would rapidly change all that.

Consular life in Trieste was, and no doubt still is, convivial and it did not surprise me in the slightest on entering the British Consulate a few days after my visit to Banfield to be offered a glass of rather good vintage champagne. The reason for this celebration was, I was told, the Conservative victory at the general election (it was 1979). Always brought up to regard politics as a corrupt profession of little interest or merit, I had to confess that the implications of the election result were lost on me. But if I missed the significance of this development, it was clear five months later that it had also not been interpreted correctly by the locally employed consular staff so busy toasting Mrs Thatcher's health on that sunny day. One of the first cuts of what later was to be dubbed the Iron Lady's swingeing axe was directed at the Foreign Office's consulates, many of which, including Trieste, were told to close by the autumn.

The British Consulate was then housed in a tall 1930s brick building at the end of the Canale Grande, not far from the crisp white façade of the Greek Orthodox church and the then fading stuccoed interior of the Café Tommaseo. As in all great Central European cities, some remnants of café life continue to flourish in Trieste. Tommaseo's, the favourite meeting place of James Joyce and his protégé Ettore Schmitz, or Italo Svevo as he was known to his readers, has been unsympathetically restored in recent months but ten years ago it possessed an extraordinary air of faded and literally crumbling grandeur.

On more than one occasion a group of octogenarian men and women, mostly writers or poets, would gather here to discuss ideas of philosophy and literature in one of six or seven of the languages they had all mastered so easily. Many of them were Jews and a reminder like the vast and impressive Byzantine synagogue a few streets away that Trieste's Jewish population had once been a considerable force in the city's commercial life. Like the British, Greeks and Serbs who settled in the city the Jews had been attracted by the enormous commercial potential of a port which had to satisfy the demands of all twenty peoples of the Habsburg Empire.

Giorgio Voghera, the octogenarian Triestine writer who can still be found at his table each morning, reading the papers and debating ideas with his friends who, like him, were also born during the days of the Habsburg Empire, still recalls the time when Trieste was a flourishing port. All the streets of the so-called Maria Theresa Quarter were lined as they are today by large neo-classical palazzi whose ground floors were in effect vast warehouses for goods bought off the ships. 'You could smell coffee, oranges and all kinds of exotic fruits depending on which ships had docked. Trieste was also the gateway to the Orient with Turkish and Montenegrin costumes rubbing shoulders with sombre-suited Triestine merchants. Every day you could see at least a dozen people wearing a fez.' Like the hero of an Italo Svevo novel, Signor Voghera though now a writer had begun his working life as an insurance clerk for Lloyds Adriatico. 'My first job was to walk from one office to the next informing the manager when the shipments of bananas had arrived.'

In those days Trieste was linked to Vienna by no fewer than three railway lines, including, as Giorgio Voghera pointed out to me, the spectacular Pontebba railway constructed through the wild rocky ravine of the Fella to Chiusaforte, names reminiscent of the tremendous Alpine struggle between the Italians and Austrians in the First World War. Whichever way one travels from Trieste, one encounters the place-names of that fearful war, the only formal modern conflict fought at high altitudes in the heart of Europe. To the west, the great rivers debouch on to the Venetian plain ringing out, like battle-honours, Tagliamento, Isonzo and of course the Piave, which as the great carved piece of rock facing the railway line proclaims in excitable script is '*Il Fiume Sacro della Patria*'. Here, if nowhere else, the Italian front in the First World War stood firm against the 'Austrogoths' as Rome dubbed the Austrians. To the east the bleak Karst or Carso still appears as Schinkel described it, 'a place which has suffered the most horrible revolutions of this earth'.

At this stage, the reader may wonder whether Trieste is not a city frozen in time, inhabited exclusively by old people. Economic decline has certainly forced the younger Triestines to move out of the city and find employment in other parts of Italy. But even among the young who remain, there is a definite feeling abroad that it is only the older generation which is capable of enjoying itself. Unlike Austrian cities, where pensioners are often regarded as a troublesome and all too vociferous minority, in Trieste there is a feeling almost of reverence when Triestines talk of their grand-parents. Certainly, for me, the hospitality of that generation was unrivalled. Perhaps as societies progress, they lose something of their openness towards strangers. Perhaps pressures of time, work and competition, the paraphernalia of success on which modern society places such value has robbed younger Triestines of their unique inheritance.

One October morning after I returned from a long boat trip to Istria, Blanka appeared in the study with a distinct expression of anticipation. 'My boy, we are off.' I had planned to catch Voghera for thirty minutes over coffee, lunch with a friend and then practise the horn for an hour but this was all to be postponed for another day as Blanka announced that she had secured invitations for a lunch party at Duino, the magnificent castle overlooking the sea along the coast.

Duino, which on the railway line to Venice is reached a few minutes after Miramar, the exotic white castle of the ill-fated Emperor Maximilian of Mexico, was of course even then a familiar landmark. I knew that it was the ancestral home of the Thurn und Taxis family who had grown rich by operating the Habsburg's first postal service. But thanks to my devotion from an early age to the cause of unrequited love and hopeless passions, I was also aware that it was where the great Austrian poet Rainer Maria Rilke composed his famous *Elegies*.

'We will look down from the Salon and see the cliffs sheer below,' Blanka remarked enthusiastically, adding tersely as I set up my music stand, 'Put away your "corn"', as she called my horn, 'and clean the shoes. The bus leaves in ten minutes.'

The road from Trieste, unlike the dramatic railway line, runs low along the cliffs passing the white turreted Miramar and its park of South American trees and exotic plants, the shortly-to-be executed Maximilian's last gift to the castle he created but was destined never to enjoy.

Beyond Miramar the cranes and shipyards of Monfalcone dis-figure the horizon, where the view should be the uninterrupted line of the beginning of the lagoons. Most of the gaunt silhouette of Duino Castle looks west, rather than east back towards Trieste and Istria, and one wonders if Rilke's verses could have been quite so evocative had he been compelled to write them gazing across the water towards modern Monfalcone. Through the old masonry of the castle's outer walls, with the sun powerfully illuminating the lush vegetation. Monfalcone was banished again from sight as we mounted a remarkable oval staircase reputed to be the work of Palladio.

At lunch the most memorable figure apart from the Prince, our host, a fine man with a rather medieval face, was a tall silver-haired man in a pinstriped suit who entered the room carrying an Italian newspaper folded neatly as if he were about to take the tube to the City. He was introduced to me as a German who was very 'Anglophile'. The reason for this and perhaps for his upright appearance emerged as he revealed that he was a Cambridge man who had been at Trinity in the 1930s. Later, I was to meet in Vienna other Central Europeans who had been to Oxford or Cambridge before the war. The combination of German lineage and an English education produced a type which was at once recognisable: English mannerisms, an open and certainly sharp mind, but all encased in an unusually formidable frame. As Blanka pointed out to me, 'He looks English, perhaps, but definitely German. Look at the size of his head.' (It was Blanka's belief that the English were distinguished from the Germans by their smaller and generally finer heads.)

With Rilke scribbling his elegies in Duino, Joyce and Svevo in Trieste, this part of Italy enjoys a literary Parnassus. The mixture of a maritime climate, fresh air and, above all, time to enjoy the contrasting cultures of the Balkans on the one hand, Central Europe and Venice on the other, all gave Trieste an advantage few other cities in Europe enjoyed when it came to the pursuit of literature. And yet, with all this beauty and civilisation, where could the inspiration have come from for Rilke's 'terrifying angels', Joyce's dark heroes of *Ulysses*?

Trieste, it must be said, like all places has its sinister side. Not for nothing have the white turrets of Miramar been described as resembling on certain days, when the cloud is low, a set of menacing teeth. When the Bora blows for more than two days and chains are erected at street corners to prevent pedestrians being blown into the road or sea, the headaches many Triestines suffer can provoke disturbing thoughts. It is then, I was assured, only a fool who walks on the Karst, which more than ever resembles a lunar landscape. The horned vipers which are to be found in the curious depressions in its rocks, the limestone dolines, are known to be at their most aggressive on such days, especially in the last hour before dusk, while below, the deserted streets, empty of noise but for the howling wind and banging shutters, take on a far from benign aspect. The dilapidated houses of the old town even lose their most faithful tenants as the Triestine cats vanish into the night.

2 DREAMERS IN CROATIA

From Trieste, the railway runs to Zagreb painfully slowly. It may be recalled by those who enjoy thrillers that it was here in the Karst landscape between Trieste and Zagreb that the Orient Express broke down in the snow and M. Henri Poirot solved his most celebrated murder case.

Today the Orient Express neglects the Karst, preferring the luxury of Vienna and Venice to the trials of Jugoslavia. For days friends warned me against taking the train. Blanka's lawyer, an ebullient and charming man who frequently visited Croatia, offered the following advice: 'They call it the most open frontier in Europe but everyone has to wait at least an hour if they go in an Italian car or train. Take the Jugoslav bus.'

If Trieste's railway station still exudes imperial grace, there are few more dingy parts of the city than the neighbouring bus station, a low-roofed building erected with the grim and ultimately shallow pomp of the Mussolini era. Nonetheless, from here, perched high, as on an American Greyhound coach, the journey to Zagreb can begin and be concluded in a fraction of the time of the combined efforts of the Jugoslav and Italian state railways. Frontier facilities still leave something to be desired. Jugoslav customs officials on the lookout for jeans, bubble-gum and other subversive materials which are in their view undermining their economy spare none of the luggage of their compatriots. The Italians on board also are given short shrift which only confirms their worst suspicions of the Slovenes, whose men patrol the frontier at this point.

Unlike the Slovenes, the Croats however appear to enjoy a degree of respect among the eastward-bound Italians. A shared Mediterranean culture, the joint history of Dalmatia and, perhaps most significantly, the absence of any present-day tensions between Croats and Italians have almost persuaded them to link hands over a sea of Slovene sullenness. However disagreeable the frontier crossing, thoughts of Zagreb banished all resentment. I was intrigued not for the last time at the strange fascination the city holds over Latin minds. Certainly the Croats are a people with a history which reflects all too well the turbulence and violence of Balkan events.

In Trieste, my first acquaintance with the Croats had been in the fascinating rooms of the Scaramanga family museum above the Austrian Consulate on the Canale Grande. For years the curator of this remarkable collection of relics of a Triestine merchant's past had been a short dark-haired elderly lady with a square-cut face and high cheek-bones. Blanka, who had spent some time in Zagreb before the war, always held her up as a typical example of the Croatian woman. Strong, devout and capable, she was an *edle Frau*, the highest compliment in Blanka's well-stocked vocabulary of superlatives. 'Good soldiers, loyal soldiers', was her general view of the Croats. The fighting qualities of the Croats together with their Catholicism have made some travellers think of Poland when visiting Croatia. Marshal Marmont, the gifted French general who during the Napoleonic Wars ruled Croatia and the rest of what Napoleon organised into the Illyrian states, described the Croats not as a nation but as 'one vast armed camp'.

For centuries the Croats shouldered the burden of that extraordinary feature of Habsburg geography, the 'Military Frontier', which ran from Transylvania to Bosnia. Along this line between Christendom and the Turk which marked the Habsburgs' eastern front, fighting was ruthless and continual. Every Croat family was organised into a military community in which to disobey an officer was to risk almost certain execution. So continual was the fighting that the head of each family was soon covered with glory, not least because the Croats were not loathe to adopt harsh methods in dealing with enemies who granted no quarter. To the Croats must fall not only the distinction of repelling the Muslim hordes eastwards through the Balkans, but also of being the first soldiers in the so-called civilised era of warfare in the eighteenth century to adopt the tactics of scorched-earth campaigning. Marmont describes well in his memoirs how nothing pleased the Croat soldiers of the frontier more than to be given torches to burn Bosnian villages.

For an Empire which had faced virtual extinction when its capital was besieged by the Turk in 1689, this rough policy might perhaps be understood. In any event, so frequently and zealously did the Croat soldiers carry out their duty that almost every community leader was ennobled by the Empire and the Croatian nobility, the closest the Austrians ever had to a Prussian *Junker* class, was well established by the time of the Napoleonic Wars, with names which even today ring of battle: Jellačič von Buzim; Špun von Strizič; Tresčec von Branski.

Both in the First and Second World War the Croats again took up arms with relish. Many more Serbs were slaughtered by the Croats who served the evil Nazi puppet regime of Ante Pavelič than by the Germans. Today, nearly fifty years after the event, these are old wounds which threaten at any moment to be reopened with disastrous consequences for the finely balanced federal system which Marshal Tito constructed out of post-war Jugoslavia.

But if the Croats were the Habsburgs' most loyal soldiers, Zagreb was never an Austrian Berlin. The city is one of the most beautiful in the Balkans and has such a civilised aspect that it can rightly claim to have one foot squarely in Central Europe. Since the unhappy conversion of Prague's gas-lamps to electricity a few years ago, Zagreb is now the only city in Mitteleuropa to be lit by that soft green light which Robert Louis Stevenson so sagely defended as 'mild old lustre'. The wisdom of the Croats in preserving this lighting instead of the nightmarish glare which has become, certain streets of London, Warsaw and Berlin excepted, the inescapable accompaniment of all evening strolls, is immediately apparent to anyone wandering about the upper town after dark. But then the Croats are dreamers, with all the sentimentality which is so often the reverse of the coin of physical cruelty.

Whether one arrives by train or bus one's first view of the city is of the square bounded on one side by the imposing Beaux-Arts railway station, on another by the equally opulent House of Artists and on a third by the splendid façade of the Hotel Esplanade, where an old-fashioned service still prevails. If in Trieste I had been surprised by the frequency of German words in the local dialect, in Zagreb it appeared that German, in particular Austrian German, had taken root in an extravagant fashion. '*Ist gefällig*', bowed the waiter after placing a cup of Turkish coffee on my table. 'To serve or to lead', Marshal Marmont's words came ringing back at the sight of a veritable army of footmen, all immaculately uniformed, pacing the foyer of the Esplanade where photographs of Josephine Baker and King Alexander recalled the hotel's heyday in the 1930s.

Through the park the Strossmajer Art Gallery also underlined what a Croat friend, Joško, said was most important to Zagreb's and therefore all Croats' souls: the sense of belonging to Europe. Joško, six foot six with a serious face and a long thin nose which befitted his career as a love-struck tenor in operettas and which appeared permanently frozen in an expression of appropriately wistful longing, was an old friend. For a year he had sung in the Ljubljana Opera House while I had attempted to reconcile an ephemeral passion for a Slovene girl in the *corps de ballet* with earning a living as a horn player.

Only those who have enjoyed the delights (and the frustrations) of the professional musician can perhaps understand the tremendous cameraderie which exists between musicians in minor opera houses. Joško, whom I was visiting now on his home territory for the first time, was as ever slightly melancholy. He agreed that Zagreb was a Balkan city but that greater Balkanisation was ruining the city and Croat nationalism remained still suppressed by petty rules and regulations imposed by Serbs in Belgrade. 'You know?' he said, quickly throwing off his reverie, 'They even wanted to ban ... ban!' (an intake of breath) '*Zrinski* ... our great national opera!'

Count Zrinski, with whose name I had first become acquainted on the bottles of brandy named after him which lined the Ljubljana Opera House bar, was a typical Croat hero and inevitably a soldier. Dashing, good-looking with the fine busby and fur-lined coat which was the traditional costume of the Croatian Bans, or governors, his exploits against the Hungarians, as the leader of a Croat national rebellion in the eighteenth century, were heady stuff for a composer to come to grips with.

The plot of *Zrinski* was, Joško assured me, 'a little thin', but no opera was ever better received in the handsome yellow stuccoed Croatian National Theatre, especially when during the last act the Croatian flag is unfurled on stage by the soldiers and the audience, as Joško related with a gleam in his eye, 'burst into wild applause'. For the authorities in Belgrade such feelings however provoked unease, for Zagreb's Croat nationalism was not only suspect in theatres.

20

In 1971 Marshal Tito moved swiftly to defuse Croat separatist feeling and purged the entire party apparatus in Zagreb of anyone found 'guilty' of 'anti-Jugoslav' tendencies. Those in cultural posts were in no way immune and the conflict involved that inevitable receptacle of nationalist spirit in any country ruled by communists, the Church. In the twin-pinnacled Catholic cathedral high up on the old town hill, there are poignant reminders of the unavoidable and tortuous struggle which Catholicism must wage against communism. In a small side chapel to the left of the main aisle lies the body of Cardinal Aloysius Stepinac, the man who more than any other in Jugoslavia came to symbolise in a later age the problems not only of a Catholic in a godless state but also of the uneasy relationship between Serbs and Croats in post-war Jugoslavia.

Stepinac first served as a priest with the Serbian army during the First World War. That he did this was proof enough of his pro-Jugoslav sentiments, but after the Second World War Marshal Tito had him tried and imprisoned on trumped-up charges and he ended his days under house arrest in 1960. But as a gesture towards the Croats, the Marshal allowed his body to be buried in Zagreb Cathedral where it remains a shrine at the foot of which scores pray daily. Perhaps because Catholicism is on the defensive here it is more impressive than in Austria or Italy. The silent worshippers, rosaries in hand, who file past Stepinac's tomb under the austere busts of the Bans and the generals who for so long guarded Christendom against non-believers, express a fervour which is lacking in countries where Catholicism reigns free.

Not far from the cathedral is the Stone Gate, a remarkable passageway which ceases for a few yards to be a busy cobbled street and becomes suddenly a candle-lit blackened tunnel with rows of Croat peasant women kneeling in pews praying in front of a Madonna. It is a remarkable shrine, in a twilight world. In one corner a plump busy lady, her face deeply lined like a mud pack which has melted in the rain, busies herself clearing piles of wax which the constant faint breeze causes to accumulate against the candles. In another corner the ceaseless murmurings of the rosaries mingle with footsteps of passers-by who find themselves without warning in what is, to all intents and purposes, a church.

Round the corner from here, I met Blanka, who was in Zagreb to visit her sister, talking in front of a fine gothic church with a riotous roof of coloured tiles to a bewildered policeman on duty outside the party headquarters. In a fruity and no doubt colourful Croatian, she was, to the man's obvious unease, frequently calling him '*Gospodin*' (Sir) instead of 'comrade', and asking him about a fire.

'Fire? Which fire? Where?' He fingered his holster nervously. 'The fire of the uprising,' explained Blanka, leaving the man even more worried. 'The fire of Matyas Gubac,' Blanka finally reassured him, enjoying his discomfort with growing amusement. 'Oh that fire, why didn't you say you meant a fire of more than five centuries ago?' The policeman looked relieved, pointing to the spot on the square where Gubac, another Croat hero who led a peasant revolt, was burned to death.

The spot almost faces the beautiful church of St Mark where the walls must have been blackened by the flames. Blanka had wanted to show me the interior and in particular a striking statue by the great Croat sculptor Mestrovič. After a dimly lit service in which the small congregation of barely a score of women sang several melodious hymns in two-part harmony, a small nun opened a side chapel to reveal a magnificent figure of a Croat woman and her child. There is much late nineteenth-century elegance in Zagreb, and its earlier Biedermeier houses in the upper town are unrivalled in Jugoslavia. But, though no modern Jugoslav guidebook mentions him – no doubt again for nationalist reasons – the outstanding art to be found here must be that of Mestrovič. The Croats themselves know this – he was after all a Croat – and they lose no time in pointing out his work and his museum, which for some curious reason does not merit even a mention in the latest Jugoslav Library's *Handbook of National Monuments of Art*.

Blanka, who had known Mestrovič briefly, was quite reserved about his talents, but she valued his art enough to visit his former home as often as she could. This ivy-covered house is now Zagreb's least known but perhaps most rewarding museum. 'Look at his women,' Blanka said, keenly eyeing as we entered the house a vast marble nude. 'This is the Croat woman. Long strong limbs, a pious jaw and a straight Illyrian nose. He has made her a barbarian, it is true,' Blanka said, stroking the statue's white curves, 'but a noble and intelligent barbarian.'

A shepherd of peasant stock born in a remote village in Dalmatia in 1883, Mestrovič can truly be said to have absorbed the spirit of his land. When he exhibited in London in 1915 art critics enthused over his stern emotions captured in the 'hard light of Dalmatia's rocky wilderness'. 'Balkan to the core,' was the verdict of Stanley Casson, while the illustrious *Studio* magazine praised Mestrovič's 'severity of lines', comparing his early work with that of Giotto. Mestrovič first worked as a sculptor in the glorious city of Spalato (now called Split), where the entire old town is hewn out of the Emperor Diocletian's former palace. From there, he moved, like so many artistically gifted people, from the outer reaches of the Empire to the only city which could develop and fashion his talents, Vienna. There, he met other Slavs studying the fine arts but more importantly he also came across Rodin and developed a strong dislike for the Italian Renaissance, preferring the Byzantine tradition of his own world.

'At heart,' wrote Casson, 'he is the child of that strange amalgam of heroism and barbarism which is the spirit of the Balkans.' Mestrovič was also something of a maverick classicist, choosing the use of orders rather than pure abstract forms. At a time when most of his contemporaries were moving in an entirely different direction, Mestrovič was reinterpreting an ancient beauty, breathing new life into old forms. Perhaps, inevitably, like all artists who follow their instincts rather than fashion, he has been confined to semi-obscurity. That such judgement is unmerited is clear as soon as one enters that small house in Zagreb. The exquisite *Girl Violinist* shows that he is a far cry from the mediocre Stalinist sculptors who replaced him in communist Jugoslavia and whose talent was limited only to constructing vast blocks of party propaganda.

The rooms are largely unchanged here; the dark varnished furniture and wooden staircase all exude an air of pre-war Zagreb. Apart from us and the young girl at the door gazing dreamily at black-and-white postcards, no one entered these rooms during the hour we wandered among the marble blocks and framed catalogues of the great man's early exhibitions. There are other museums in Zagreb, notably the Strossmajer Art Gallery near the railway station and the old town museum beneath the cathedral, to say nothing of the extraordinary Mimara Collection housed in a school near the opera house. But anyone wishing to understand Croatia and breathe something of the Croat spirit must first go to Mestrovič's house beyond St Mark's church.

After Mestrovič the enormous Mimara Collection, named after one of the most bizarre art collectors of the twentieth century, comes as a shock. It is just as well that this vast assembly of art from all ages is situated a tram ride away to the west beyond the opera house. Of Mimara little but rumour is known. It seems certain that his real name was Ante Topič, and he may well have been a close friend and art adviser of Adolf Hitler's. One thing is certain, he knew a lot about art and how to acquire it. When he died in 1985, he left 'millions of pounds' worth of art treasures to the Jugoslav government on condition that it would be exhibited in his native Croatia. Since 1987 it has been on show in the lavish new gallery converted from a former Austro-Hungarian high school.

The Mimara Collection is a puzzle. There are Reynolds, Van Dycks, Rembrandts, exquisite Bohemian crystal, Bronze Age and Roman relics. Some are undoubtedly forgeries: but all? 'Forgeries or not,' said Joško passionately, 'it reminds us that we are linked with Europe. We are closer to this art than the South.'

In the Gradska Kavana on the Trg Republica, a grand café which like the city it is in is neither wholly Balkan nor entirely Central European, these sentiments were reinforced. The coffee is Turkish but the long curves of the staircase breathe a Central European art-deco while around the marble tables gather old men in suits with ties, impeccably dressed, engaging in quiet conversation one moment, retreating behind newspapers the next. In the summer there are scores of tables placed outside on the end of the large empty space which though now called Republic Square once commemorated another Croatian hero whose name like that of Mestrovič is missing from so many modern Jugoslav guides to the city.

For nearly a hundred years, Jellačič Square had been at the heart of Zagreb, epitomising in its name the aspirations, loyalty and courage of the Croat nation, then ruled by the Hungarians. At the centre of the square stood the bronze equestrian statue of Croatia's greatest governor and Ban: Baron Josef Jellačič von Buzim (1801–59).

But Jellačič's sword pointed towards Hungary, the country which in 1848 rose up in open rebellion against its Habsburg rulers. The combination of Croatia's resentment of Hungarian rule and

Jellačič's personal loyalty to the House of Habsburg drove him to help Vienna subdue the Magyar revolutionaries. Not surprisingly such a symbol of imperialism, combining as it did Croat nationalism and aggression towards 'a brother socialist land', was suspect in Marshal Tito's eyes and the statue was carted away, its loss lamented to this day by Croats old and young alike.

Who was this man though, whose name and image posed such a threat to the fledgling Jugoslav state that both had to be suppressed? Born the son of a soldier on the Military Frontier, Jellačič was what perhaps only a Croat and a Pole can be among the Slav nations of Europe, a soldier through and through. A short man, broad-shouldered and vigorous, his thick, dark eyebrows gave him a somewhat stern expression which a prominent nose, big moustache and firmly cleft chin did not altogether belie.

'There was something fierce in his appearance,' an old man born under the Austrian Empire before the First World War and whose grandfather had served under Jellačič, explained in the Gradska Kavana. 'Fierce; but gentle.' The old man leant forward on the stick firmly planted between two stocky legs. 'His brown eyes could look tender or flash fiercely. His black thick hair was receding from his temples and his forehead was high and open,' he continued, half in a trance. It was almost as if he spoke from personal memory.

In the only second-hand bookshop of any merit in Zagreb, a portrait of the Ban resplendent in Imperial white, the Grand Cross of the Order of Maria Theresa proudly displayed on his chest, shows an intelligent and not insensitive face. Dark by nature, long service had clearly tanned his complexion, leaving the decisive lines of a commander upon his face. Those who were his contemporaries were impressed by his voice which could sound at once low and sharp and also ring clearly with compelling force. In society he was quick-witted and charming. In private, like many Slavs, he was quiet, very simple and almost sad as depression and gloom encompassed him on occasions.

This temperament, so very Croat, meant that he was much more than a soldier who had mastered the art of the Empire's frontier warfare, which in its savagery and unpredictability matched that of the Great Game fought by the British along the Khyber Pass. A gifted poet, he had at an early age been sent at Imperial request to the Theresianum Academy in Vienna. A love of languages – he spoke German as well as Croatian– meant that he combined two qualities formidable in any age but in the turbulent years of the 1840s the very key to power: soldierly courage and statesmanlike oratory.

In 1848, when revolution was overtaking almost every city of the Empire, Jellačič became the man of the hour, catapulted into centre stage by events and the sudden rise of Croat nationalism demanding leaders who were masters of their own tongue as well as German. As Croatia was then ruled by Hungary this nationalism was fought tooth and nail even by the new republican liberals installed in Budapest after the revolution. That Jellačič was capable of dealing with the Hungarians in terms of oratory as well as arms was demonstrated by his extraordinary appearance before the Habsburg court removed, for reasons of safety in 1848, to Innsbruck. The Emperor Franz Josef declared in front of the entire court and diplomatic corps, after being bullied by the Hungarian nobles, that attempts to sever Croatia from Hungary were unacceptable. The Croat delegation listened in silence, noting the smirk of Count Esterhazy standing behind the throne, but their Ban was equal to the emergency. It was his right to answer and defend himself, and his words were ready, quick and above all clear; very far from the courtier-like subservience of the Hungarians, yet with a soldierly obedience to superiors in every tone.

From the blunt soldierly beginning, 'Sire, I ask Your Majesty's pardon but I wish to save the Empire,' to the cry from the heart one hour later, 'These gentlemen may live if they wish when the Empire has fallen but I – I cannot,' the General held the court spellbound. Such oratory repeated on the square which was to bear his name, in front of his own people, only fell on more fertile ground and no man's name carried more respect among the Croats than Jellačič's. Moreover, if contemporary sources are to be believed, Jellačič belonged to that small group of war leaders who were apparently invulnerable in battle. He never shirked leading from the front and being with his men in the thick of the fighting while officers and horses fell by the dozen at his side. Jellačič appeared to lead a charmed life. In engagements against the Hungarian revolutionaries in 1848–9 he proved his dash and coolness a hundred times.

Today his statue lies hidden in some remote part of his city. No one will say where it is but all agree that it could never have been destroyed. 'They would never have allowed it to be broken up. No Croat would have permitted this,' my old friend in the Gradska Kavana assured me. 'The politicians need it. One day it will come back, though who knows if the sword will still be pointing towards Hungary,' he added, a twinkle in his eye.*

And so Zagreb and Croatia sleep like sleeping beauties awaiting a kiss from Prince Charming. Their history and their heroes alike are hidden from all but the most enquiring minds. On the crisp bright winter afternoons with skies a bright blue and the view from the upper town to the distant hills as clear as any Tibetan vista, Zagreb is silent as only a Slav city can be. From Maximir Park in the suburbs to the peaceful village of Samobor on the road to Ljubljana, the stillness is inescapable. On such a day, in a small house up in the cobbled streets beyond St Mark's church, Blanka took me to tea with a Countess Kukuljević, an ageing and handsome lady whose great-grandfather had, in 1848, been part of Jellačič's council and whose love of the Croat language had inspired him to express in literary form the powerful belief of the time that ancient Illyria could be reborn, with Zagreb as its capital.

At a time when the Hungarian Diet showed only pride and arrogance towards the Slav deputies from Croatia, the idea of Illyria was a powerful one. Magyar attempts to replace Croat with Hungarian as the official language of Croatia only fuelled interest in this romantic idea. Kukuljević took his cue from Ljudevic Gaj, a Croat writer who seized on the idea of sudden Slav unity founded on language. From southern Styria down to Montenegro and Serbia, he saw all the Slav provinces close to the Adriatic joined in a 'Great Illyrian brotherhood'. Illyria as a name for the movement had a fine romantic sound and with another Croat noble, Count Draškovič, Kukuljević appealed above all to that last court of any young nation: its women, 'the noble daughters of Illyria'. The Croat women, who had astounded ancient chroniclers with their fierceness against the enemy, would now channel their energies towards developing the Croat language and instilling it in their children.

---

*Indeed forty-four years after the Communists dragged it away, the statue is due to be re-erected by the end of 1990, the result of old passions again stirring in the Balkan world.

27

The reaction of the Hungarians to this cause was predictable. While they derived from Vienna liberty for themselves, no such freedom was to be granted to the Croat lands which they so poorly ruled. The haughtiness of the Magyars which has so often disfigured their history, casting a dark shadow over their other more bracing qualities, was never more apparent than in the fierce debate of the Pressburg Diet where, in the face of ridicule from the Magyar leaders, it was left to Kukuljević to stand up and warn sagely: 'Gentlemen. Hungary is an island surrounded by a Slav sea whose waves are rising. Do not be surprised if you find yourselves shortly drowning in it.'

Croatia's freedom was not to come for another two generations. The Habsburgs' policy of divide and rule ensured that Jellačič was deprived of the great prize of Croatian independence which he felt was a just reward for supporting Austria. Like the loyal servant he was, he never allowed his betrayal to embitter him.

Between the wars Zagreb became the second city of Jugoslavia and by far the country's most European metropolis, but the ethnic conflicts which pitted Croat against Serb so mercilessly during the Second World War inevitably destroyed Croatia's dignity.

Countess Kukuljević's rooms, like those of Blanka's sister, belied any hint that decades of communism had ravaged the spirit of the Croat nobility. A young housekeeper showed us into a vast salon with magnificent portraits of uniformed Kukuljevičs gazing sternly down at a table laid for a sumptuous tea. Conversation in Italian, German and English as well as Croat followed on a range of themes which tried to the limits my knowledge of music, art and history. Then, as the shutters were half drawn the whole room suddenly became bathed in the mellow gold of the January Croatian sun. Both ladies lay down on separate sofas to rest, the silence unbroken save for the tic-toc of a carriage clock and the distant rustling of dead leaves in the garden below.

3 THE PEARLS OF ILLYRIA

The sights of Fiume, so Paget wrote in 1839, are no great matter. Rijeka, as we must call Fiume today, has none of the charm of Trieste though its situation, with the islands of the Quarnero to the west and the mountains to the east, gives it a certain drama which is absent from its Italian neighbour.

One cannot easily forget the railway from Zagreb with its spectacular cuttings and descents. But the most picturesque route to the Adriatic is the line from Ljubljana, past the small village which has surely the most romantic of names on the Karst: Illirska-Bistrica. As the train careers madly down the harsh rocky landscape this name should not be forgotten, for we are indeed heading for Illyria. If today the great port of Rijeka leaves us as cold as it did Paget over a hundred years ago, it should be noted that no one can begin to understand this city without stumbling across the name of the man who took an altogether different and more romantic view of the shabby nineteenth-century buildings clustered around this harbour.

It is the fate of Gabriele d'Annunzio, the frenzied Italian poet of the early years of this century, to be better remembered by some for his politics than for his poetry. 'Every man regrets not being a soldier', wrote Dr Johnson, and for all we know this feeling may well have afforded d'Annunzio an extreme discomfiture which the pen alone could not relieve.

The end of hostilities in 1918 gave rise to a peculiarly awkward situation at Fiume. The port, though fraudulently annexed to Hungary in 1868, only possessed a small and artificial Magyar population. The number of Italians according to the Austrian census was 24,212 in 1910, while Croats made up 13,350 of the city's inhabitants. The city's hinterland however was Croat, even though the city was, with its shutters and classical architecture, thoroughly Italian in character, and indeed bore then as now no small resemblance to Trieste's urban aspect. Herein lay the inescapable seeds of ethnic conflict. At the Peace Conference in Versailles, Italian claims met with a solid refusal from the American President Wilson. Meanwhile the Croats and Serbs of the new Jugoslav kingdom saw their port, as it seemed to them – for they had freely used it for centuries – becoming increasingly remote and alien.

It was at this juncture, with passions running high, Serbian soldiery on the outskirts of the city and an Italian warship anchored offshore, that the poet-aviator made his dramatic entry on to the Adriatic stage. In September 1919, assembling with a band of black-cloaked volunteer desperadoes like the chorus in an early Verdi opera, he flew from Ronchi (*dei Legionari*) near Trieste and seized Fiume in the name of Italy.

This swashbuckling adventure, forever remembered in the annals of modern Italian history, only served however to unite all the Slavs passionately against the Italians, as Serbs, Croats and Slovenes forgot their ancient differences in the face of the common foe. By the Treaty of Rapallo in 1920 Fiume suffered the unhappy fate of all cities with ethnic conflict and became a 'Free Port'. After the Second World War it was returned to Croatia and became the most important commercial harbour of communist Jugoslavia.

If, at times, the shabbiness of Rijeka appears particularly oppressive after Trieste it is well to recall that the expulsion and humiliation of the middle classes – any communist's first target – was reinforced here with virulent anti-Italian feeling. The Italian merchants and white-collar workers were seen as guilty on two counts, as both the racial and the class enemy. Retribution was exacted with a double vigour from which Rijeka today has still to recover.

These grim thoughts crossed my mind as I found myself staring at what must be the only opera house in the world built overlooking a half-derelict shipyard. Even Trieste's maritime Teatro Verdi is flanked on the Riva by other impressive classical buildings a good half mile from the port. Here, however, those two prolific Austrian architects Helmer and Fellner, responsible for opera houses in virtually every city of the Habsburg Empire, chose in 1908 a site which is as eccentric and wilful as anything a modern architect might select.

Admittedly, Baedeker suggests that in 1908 this small area close to the Porto Baross was quite civilised. Perhaps Helmer and

Fellner's vast neo-rococo building appeared then less out of place than it does today, but even Baedeker cannot conceal that it is situated opposite the fishmarket and surrounded on three sides by water and on the fourth by railway tracks. Gustav Mahler, who made his early career conducting in Ljubljana and Trieste, often complained of the railway traffic which kept him awake outside the Hotel de la Ville in Trieste. History does not relate whether stirring performances of Verdi in Fiume were given an extra piquancy by the audible crash of goods wagons rumbling past the theatre across the Canale della Fiumana.

Its unusual site aside, it must be said that the opera house here is in every other way a civilised establishment. The singers drawn from the dwindling Fiumani sing their Verdi and Puccini in Italian, though occasionally a guest Madam Butterfly from Zagreb will answer Lieutenant Pinkerton's Latin advances in earthy Croat. Among the audience of this opera house, which sadly is rarely filled to capacity these days, there is sometimes an English or Scottish voice to be heard: a daughter of a retired British consul; the wife of a Dalmatian merchant seaman. Whatever the tortuous history of local ethnic rivalries, Rijeka, like every other great eastern Adriatic port, welcomes the stranger from afar as best it can.

For some reason, perhaps because of its maritime situation, every time I have visited Rijeka the opera company has been performing *Madam Butterfly*. It is, I was assured by a severe but helpful Scottish lady sitting next to me in the stalls, the 'house favourite', but even had I been tone deaf or weary of Puccini I would not have regretted entering the house which boasts, unique among the former opera houses of the Austrian Empire, several frescos by Gustav Klimt. They are, it must be conceded, not his most characteristic work. The voluptuousness which was to make him so infamous in Vienna is here only hinted at, but the Adriatic air and the proximity to the legendary beauties of Dalmatia clearly inspired the artist to produce images which are a welcome distraction from the scene of violence and fraught emotions towards the end of the drama on stage.

Though there are delicious strawberries in the market and an imposing fortress, once the home of yet another Irishman who served the Habsburgs – a General Nugent – there is little to delay us in Rijeka. Of the café life in Trieste I saw no signs, but the ships which were so conspicuously absent in the Italian port were visible here by the score, underlining the fact that Trieste's decline has been Rijeka's gain. It is no longer possible to sail to Dalmatia in the magnificent steamers of the old Austrian-Lloyd line, those floating five-star hotels with which at least one traveller here before the First World War, Colonel Barry of the Indian Army Medical Service, was so taken that he insisted on dedicating his book of letters to them. But the fleet of the Jadrolinija is not without its charm and though we could regain Central Europe in a matter of minutes by driving from Rijeka along the coast to the delightful resort of Opatija, the former Abbazia, it is with these ships that we will continue our journey to the Balkans. The old Austrian Riviera, where marble was fashioned from straw, must be left for another day.

Without doubt it is best to take these steamers early in the season. During the summer, they are intolerably crowded, whereas before Easter on the less frequented routes such as to Rab, the old Italian island of Arbe, it is more than likely that the passengers will be outnumbered by the crew.

I know of no finer introduction to the glories of Dalmatia than this lovely island, a whiff of whose rosemary and myrtle is encountered on deck a good hour before the island swings into view. The ship in March and April often arrives in the evening and at first all that is seen in the darkness is the gaunt silhouette of several towers strangely reminiscent of San Gimignano in Tuscany. Rab, as an island of the Quarnero group, is enriched with the Venetian detailing which is now encountered all the way down to the Albanian frontier. To understand Venice fully one must first travel east through these islands to see the tremendous inspiration that the combination of inexhaustible supplies of white marble and a brilliant light gave to craftsmen and artists working in both classical and gothic idioms. Entire cities, even their pavements, were fashioned from this gleaming stone. After the squalor of modern Rijeka and even the melancholy glitter of Opatija this island opens a door into a new world all too rarely seen in the Balkans and which for a brief period affords considerable relief from the trials of travelling in this part of the world. Between here and the great bay of Cattaro, now known as Kotor, several hundred miles to the south, the inhabitants though they speak the same language as their kinsmen in Zagreb are of a different culture. Thanks to the bleak heights of the Karst mountains which run a few miles inland all the way down the Balkan peninsula, these islands and Dalmatia proper have always faced west and were able to enjoy a degree of civilisation missed by other Slavs isolated from the sea by the towering peaks. At Rab the contrast, perhaps because it is so sudden, is still by far the sweetest welcome to the lands of the Serenissima, east of Venice.

Architecturally, too, there are fine details of doors and arches which before the First World War many a draughtsman diligently sketched. The older islanders here still speak Italian and in the fields beyond the town a woman in black bombazine may well be overheard saying her prayers in the language of Rome. Out of season, the small hotels built by the Austrians are quiet; even the dull thud of the town's single discotheque is silenced after 8 p.m. In these conditions, with barely more than a few lanterns showing to guide one's steps, the place to be is the small square at the top of the old town beneath the towers.

From one side of this miniature square the drop appears sheer to the sea but it is not to the depths of the Adriatic that the eye wanders, rather it is to the sky above, ablaze with more stars than one can imagine. Is there a more brilliant night sky on the Adriatic? No doubt those who have experienced Korcula and Lokrum will advance their own claims, but on a warm and almost over-whelmingly fragrant late March evening I counted here during a single hour sixteen shooting stars and, adding their own strange mysteries to nature's silver vault, three satellites.

After Rab, the glories which followed along the Dalmatian coast crescendo relentlessly before climaxing in Dubrovnik, formerly known as Ragusa. Spectacular if less peaceful come Zadar (Zara), Šibenik (Sebenico) and Trogir (Traù). But it is not until we reach Split (Spalato) that the first acquaintance with Venice's eastern empire is overwhelmed by the new and extraordinary spectacle of a city carved out of the fabric of an imperial Roman villa. From the sea the long Doric arcade still shows the outline of the Emperor Diocletian's residence.

The experience of other ruins however exalted can in no way prepare one for Split. The heart of the city is a town carved out of a ruined palace. At virtually every corner the eye is caught by some tremendous piece of Roman masonry. Between the arches, flats and houses have appeared over the centuries and are still filled with families whose numbers if not whose noise recall the back streets of Naples. The area covered by the palace is a graduated quadrilateral of 38,236 metres; most of the 'modern' houses are five storeys high but though the 'villa' roof is gone the peristyle and the architrave with its cornice and a wealth of carved enrichments are preserved so that throughout the city ancient Ionic detailing and modern Venetian blinds can be seen cheek by jowl. No city on the Adriatic encompasses so much architectural richness; no city in Dalmatia appears more inviting to the stranger. But sadly, no city along the Jugoslav coast offers more problems to the visitor set on finding a room within its great walls. .

The former Piazza dei Signori, still unmistakably *risorgimentale* in spirit, boasts what was once a fine hotel but its dilapidated rooms invariably were long ago booked up. 'Why not try the Hotel Majestic? The Hotel Grand?' These superlatively named establishments unfortunately are all situated miles away from the *citta vecchia*, their sites being the result of a demand for sun and sand rather than history and architecture. It is a mistake I suspect the Italians, had they been allowed to remain in Dalmatia and develop its tourism, would never have made. The Croats however, no doubt 'guided' by the state apparatus, had no other option. Keep the tourists out of the city and put them all in a concrete ghetto with a beach as far away as possible. It is an error which time and again is encountered in Dalmatia and appears typical of the lack of intelligence with which tourism and indeed so much else in communist Yugoslavia has been developed.

On arriving in Split the traveller is invariably exhausted and it is an awful feat of determination to attempt somehow to secure a room in the city, but as I eventually discovered after several weary hours the password is *prenočiste*. This means some form of lodging which, not being a hotel, cannot under the absurd bureaucracy of communism strictly speaking offer rooms to foreigners. But rules when foolish are broken. The most capacious of these *prenočiste* is actually less than *due passi* away from the Golden Gate, the villa's well-preserved and lavish main entrance. Inside works a handsome young man who claims in Italian to be the *padrone* until after a few minutes' conversation a lady of vast dimensions appears to usurp this impostor and to explain that it is 'impossible' to take rooms here. They are too small, too modest and there are no bathrooms in them. 'Please go to the Majestic or the Grand,' she pleads. At this point the traveller must decide whether to argue each of these points in detail or proffer a small sum of what remains in the Balkans, whatever its fate elsewhere, the all-conquering currency and see if the rooms become more 'suitable' on receipt of a twenty-dollar bill.

The result is a delightful tour up a rickety series of steps into a spartan but clean room, simply furnished but with a view Diocletian himself might have enjoyed: the small gateway, the pieces of peristyle, the arcades and beyond the blue Adriatic. At this height the sun streams in until the late afternoon while adjoining the room is a terrace perfectly situated for the watercolourist, diarist or simple post-prandial dreamer. On reflection it is perhaps just as well that only the most determined or fortunate enjoy such a view and that most visitors to the city are forced to make their way to a bigger hotel a few miles away. Should the chance of such a room be too readily available I'm sure it would be even more difficult to secure. Nonetheless those fortunate enough to put up there must tolerate a tremendous row in the early hours of the morning, for at 5.30 a.m., amid much shouting and laughter, twelve of the city's police force billeted here head for the shower rooms with great cheer.

With the glory of Split beneath one's feet it is easy to imagine how Robert Adam, when he visited 'Spalatro', was so carried away by what he saw. Adam took to sketching everything in sight, even the corner bastions, which forced the Austrian guards to the conclusion that he must be a spy, and the great architect passed more than a few hours in custody beneath the Temple of Aesculepius whose exquisite mouldings he had spent so much time recording.

Though it is now surrounded by dingy suburbs, there is one place at least where the visitor to Split, however enchanted by his surroundings within the walls, must venture *fuori delle mura* if he is to understand fully the extraordinary views he now enjoys. It is still just about possible – but it is a dismal jaunt – to walk to Salona these days, but for those who cannot face the heat, dust and uninspiring scenery a bus can be taken from beyond the Golden Gate to the birthplace of Diocletian and the eerie remains of this city.

Diocletian was born in Salona in AD 245 and became Emperor at the age of thirty-nine, before abdicating twenty years later to cultivate cabbages a stone's throw from his birthplace. Most of the relics of Salona are now in the archaeological museum in Split but there remains here an intangible mood of reverence even if the situation of these broken columns and curious sarcophagi is no longer as unspoilt as it once was. From the date of its abandonment in the early seventh century Salona was for generations at the mercy of rains and winds. Only in 1842 did excavation begin in earnest, digging in ever-increasing circles around the mouldy tombs of Dalmatian saints and other strange Christian antiquities. The monogram of Christ is everywhere to be found between the massive sarcophagi of early Christians whom, if I have copied the inscription correctly – DEUS NOSTER PROPITIUS REIPUBLICAE ROMANAE – were not averse to praying in support of a republican form of government.

Though the eye must now avoid the western and southern aspects of the view from the once peaceful and remote Salona, to the north-east, it cannot fail to note a ruined castle on a remarkable precipice of rock guarding a solitary pass into the hinterland behind the city. There is an almost dreamlike quality to this single and rather forbidding outcrop, the site of old conflicts between the men of the coast and the men of the mountains. Today Clissa remains a strange place, apparently haunted by the ghosts of ancient discords. On a clear day the view across the hinterland describes the snow-capped peaks of Herzegovina. On a grey day under a leaden sky I know of nothing in Dalmatia which looks so sinister.

From Salona back to Split it was once possible to enjoy the Riviera dei Sette Castelli but today urban development has dwarfed what was described by more than one traveller to Dalmatia before the First World War as 'Dalmatia's string of golden pearls'. High up on a handsome road beyond the walls of Split stands however one monument, albeit more recent, which has survived. The severe classical portico of the Villa Mestrovič is a welcome reminder of that great sculptor's work. The villa is now a museum, rather better known than that in Zagreb. It contains fewer personal mementoes but many of this neglected artist's best works. His presence here among the pines reminds us of the forceful Slav character which, despite the softness of the view to the west, appears to have been moulded more under the exacting conditions of the mountains to the east.

This forcefulness, even spiritual strength, I encountered vividly a few days later on the island of Korčula. Korčula is probably the most beautiful of the Dalmatian islands. I say 'probably' because unfortunately the island of Vis, where a fine classical monument commemorates the destruction of a French fleet by an English naval officer called Hoste, is off limits for all but Jugoslav citizens and I suspect that this westernmost isle of the archipelago may hold ever greater charms.* But in Korčula, where the streets are paved with the gleaming, glaring white marble first seen on Rab, there is a fine cathedral in which until recently, no matter which day of the week one entered, one would always see in the early morning an impressive and stalwart figure polishing laboriously all the gilt and brass fittings.

Father Ivo, six foot three in his socks and, with what appears to be a glass eye, cutting a somewhat intimidating figure, is perhaps the best-known personality on the island. The trials and persecutions of the Catholic church in Croatia have been touched on in the chapter on Zagreb. In Dalmatia the post-war years brought no fewer challenges as the communists again dealt with their greatest of foes in the only way they knew and went about murdering priests. By February 1945 eight priests had been shot in Šibenik, ten in Spalato, fourteen in Dubrovnik, twenty-three in the Franciscan Province of the Redeemer and forty-five in Mostar. There was no semblance of legality about any of these executions. Some of the victims were shot on their doorsteps; others arraigned before gangs of partisan thugs; the majority though were carried off by Marshal Tito's secret police and disposed of silently. It was certainly true that many priests had supported the Croatian Catholic puppet state set up by the Nazis but others were innocent of any such associations. By 1952 it was only Evelyn Waugh who reminded England and the western world of the unpleasant affair and pointed out the bleak pattern of communist repression in Croatia and elsewhere in Jugoslavia: prohibition of religious teaching in the home and in church, crushing financial levies, closure of seminaries, expulsion of orders. Most of these restrictions are still to some extent in force today.

Partly through strength of character, and partly because unlike other priests he actually fought against the Germans, Father Ivo managed to defend his church and his devout and loyal con-

*The island is expected to be opened in 1991.

gregation from the worst excesses of the regime. Not only is his small church kept in immaculate condition, he has next to it what is the most inviting museum anywhere in Dalmatia, a treasury of Catholic relics and mementoes of Korčula's earliest days. The only souvenir postcards available are faded black-and-white photographs of a fine gothic window but, seizing my arm in a vice-like grip, Father Ivo whisked me round the collection with surprising vigour. Relics of one martyr, portraits of another; it was not until we reached a room devoted to more recent ecclesiastical works of art where hangs a large and imposing portrait of a priest in full regalia, that we drew breath. The lavish costume with biretta and cassock was at first distracting, but then I thought I recognised the expression. Father Ivo seized my arm even more tightly, looked me straight in the eye with a gaze which must have left many a parishioner shivering, and then broke into a fit of noisy and for me very welcome laughter. 'Portrait of the priest as a young man,' he boomed. He smiled and moved me on to another room. A few years later I was to hear how this brave man went on his knees each morning for hours on end until, bent with age, his massive frame finally succumbed to illness. In Dubrovnik, Zagreb and even England there were friends who had valued his guidance since childhood and who flocked to his side to pay their respects.

Elsewhere on Korčula there are several fine courtyards, in the discovery and comparison of which a pleasant morning can be spent, while the fine town walls reinforced by the French and then later by the Austrians are unrivalled except by those of Dubrovnik. Korčula is moreover unique in one curious respect, insofar as it contains the only house in Jugoslavia owned by a foreigner. Under Jugoslav law no property can be owned by anyone who does not hold Jugoslav citizenship. But Sir Fitzroy Maclean, who was Churchill's liaison officer with Marshal Tito, was rewarded for his gallant efforts by the late Marshal with a modest house here; the Jugoslav Parliament had to pass a special law to allow the baronet to take possession. Though it is rare to coincide with that distinguished gentleman's visits, few are the people on the island who do not on seeing an English face ask, 'Are you a friend of Fitzrova?'

From Korčula it is only a few hours' sailing to the pearl of the Adriatic, the ancient and most splendid city of Ragusa, which today we call Dubrovnik. As elsewhere along the Dalmatian riviera it is a noisy and busy place between Easter and October but out of season its soothing qualities are unrivalled; here if nowhere else in communist Jugoslavia is a place to iron out the creases of one's soul. Whether one stays at the largest hotel built by the Austrians, the Imperial, and until comparatively recently the only establishment of any efficiency in Dalmatia, or in the more modest but quieter 1920s Excelsior, or indeed in one of the private rooms let out in villas, the city is an oasis of calm unchanging. The Ragusans, whatever the vicissitudes of their country, still keep up old standards of courtesy almost extinct elsewhere in Jugoslavia. But to encounter such qualities at their best one must meet an old Ragusan and these as the years go by are, sadly, becoming increasingly hard to find. Here as elsewhere in the 'other' Europe it is the female of the species which is the most resilient.

On a painfully hot night, unable to sleep during my first summer visit, I walked down the Stradone, that remarkable stretch of seventeenth-century town planning which cuts through the old town from one two-foot-wide gate to another. It is always astonishing to recall that this city can only be entered through three gates, each barely wide enough to take two men abreast. At the end of this *corso*, beyond the magnificent Rector's Palace, a gap in the wall brings one to the great curved bastion which, unlit at night and with a stormy wind blowing, requires no small nerve to walk round.

Fortunately on that first hot night there was little wind by 2 a.m.; but as I crept round dwarfed by the deserted ancient masonry – then unlit save by moon and stars – with only the narrow ledge on which I stood between the towering walls and the limitless black sea, I was not a little surprised to find silhouetted against the sky an erect figure in a long coat leaning on a walking stick. As I moved forwards the figure turned to the right and, beating the stick against the ledge, moved off slowly further round the tower. As it did so I saw more clearly: an old lady, possibly seventy, probably older, with a headscarf tied so as to give her a saintly Byzantine aspect. She marched rather than walked, her stick marking time, the moonlight emphasising her deep-set eyes, high cheekbones and strong beaky nose.

Even if I had only seen her shadow and watched its gait, I don't think it would have been possible to mistake this dignified figure for a cousin of Blanka von Korvin's. The same school was written on every elegant, decisive action and gesture. As I pondered on the relative merits of silence and formal recognition, the figure suddenly turned towards me. 'What a fine night,' I stammered in Italian, '*Si, si, bella notte, ma* ... I also speak English, monsieur,' came the reply. Ksenja Treščec von Branski, the daughter of an old Croatian family ennobled by the Habsburgs as a reward for cool action on the Military Frontier in the eighteenth century, often walked out late at night. The heat of Dubrovnik in the summer within the city walls is formidable. Like many ladies of great age, she seemed to need little sleep and could be found almost every evening just before midnight picking her way through the deserted stage-set which is Dubrovnik at night.

'Look at these,' a knobbly hand clutching a stick beat against curious lumps in the paving beneath the tower. 'All the result of the earthquake,' she sighed. As we walked back along the terrace to the Stradone and the lantern illuminated my companion more clearly, I saw a thin fragile body crowned with a head of extraordinary strength. Every lined feature seemed to betray a forceful character and yet the eyes were alive with sparkle and, so reminiscent of Blanka, an almost childlike humour. 'So you wish to know about Ragusa? Well, tomorrow morning, monsieur, at nine-thirty in the Franciscan cloister and we shall begin. Good-night, monsieur.' The figure marched off, a downwards gesture of the stick preceding every step. Once again I was left in the darkness to thread my way home through the unlit streets wondering – it was after all very late – whether I had seen a ghost or had fallen asleep and dreamt.

A considerable amount of time could be spent weighing up the comparative charms of the great Franciscan cloister in Ragusa and the arcaded court of its principal rival, the Dominican order, on the other side of the town. Many a peaceful hour can be spent reading, dreaming and even sleeping (though this is not encouraged) in both of these jewels of late gothic art. I had already visited both before I met Ksenja, so I did not dawdle on my way to the Franciscan building.

It was just past 9.30 and I was beginning to wonder whether I had indeed imagined my nocturnal encounter when the tap-tap-tap of a walking stick raised my hopes and Ksenja turned a corner, leant on her stick and gazed, seemingly oblivious to my presence, at a pair of finely carved capitals. Then, 'You studied history of art, monsieur? Tell me, what date are these?' The face remained impassively regarding the white stone, the stick pointed at the third arcade along. 'Fourteenth-century?' I ventured, hoping that I had remembered Baedeker correctly. 'Correct!' came a parade-ground voice. '1317 to be precise, monsieur.' Thus began a tour which took me into palaces, churches and quite simple houses which though unadorned without, contained frescos, ornate staircases and vaulted rooms of great beauty. A herald would find unlimited scope for his curiosity in Dubrovnik; over almost every house there is the escutcheon of one of the many Ragusan families who not only spoke the finest Croat in the land but were to the last man aristocrats. Ksenja related that when in 1798 Napoleon annexed the independent republic of Ragusa to his new-found 'Kingdom of Illyria', no fewer than sixty heads of noble families committed suicide rather than live ignominiously under revolutionary rule.

What is so remarkable about all these palazzi is their understatement. Here, unlike Venice which the city resembles in so many other ways, sober self-effacement is the watchword. Ironically it is only on the vast defensive walls that are open every day until 3 p.m.– the most magnificent promenade in the Adriatic – that one realises this. For almost without exception no significant architectural adornment is visible on any of the palaces. Only near the dome of the cathedral is the eye caught by the heavy pedimented windows which mark the uniquely exuberant palazzo of a roving naval commander who in the mid-eighteenth century, inspired by Lecce, remodelled his house with a swaggering top-storey loggia so that, however difficult it is to admire it from the narrow street, his fashionable creation could still be visible from afar. Inside this palazzo, the exact location of which is not easy to find once in the maze of narrow streets to the seaward side of the Stradone, there is a fine escutcheon and more pretension in the staircase. Otherwise, cool Adriatic understatement prevails: simple forms and restrained frescos with characteristically Illyrian fragments of crude, untutored classical ornament.

As we wandered down the Stradone, Ksenja pointing out where she had seen the late Duke of Windsor as Prince of Wales dine with Mrs Simpson or where as a child her father had bought her some chocolates, older Ragusans would pass saying not '*Zdravo!*' or

'*Doberdan*', the usual greetings to be heard in Croatia, but a word which sounded rather like '*Slugace*'. This greeting, Ksenja explained, was a contraction of the old Ragusan phrase '*Slugace vam s Klanyam*', which translated in full means, 'I most humble servant bow to you'. The greeting's survival, I noted, was limited exclusively to those of Ksenja's generation, as its old-world charm cut no ice to my regret with the Amazonian blonde girl behind the ice-cream bar near the Rector's Palace.

'Things are better now than they were but when I think of my childhood!' Ksenja clasped her hands together and pursed her lips to a tight wistful smile and conversation turned towards books. Had I read *Henry Esmond*? Why not? What was I reading now? On this, my first visit to Dubrovnik, I had bought at the expense of many other books Rebecca West's formidable 700-page *Black Lamb and Grey Falcon*. This remarkable work, written just as the Germans were invading Jugoslavia, is an emotional *tour de force* which for all its wealth of information is predictably violently anti-German. In the chapter on Dubrovnik Miss West lost no opportunity to snipe at the nearest thing to the Germans which had ever descended on the Dalmatian coast before 1941, the Austrians. Not even the Empress Elizabeth, who bravely met her death at the hands of a fanatical Italian who stabbed her through the heart as she stepped off a steamer in Switzerland, is spared Miss West's criticism for having attempted to reside in Dubrovnik. 'Who is this awful lady – West?' Ksenja angrily asked when I read her the relevant passage. 'The Empress never had a villa near here and the Austrians were not the villains this foolish woman imagines.' Such was Ksenja's annoyance that I refused to read any more, but on her insistence I was forced to explain other passages which only angered her further until she shut the book exclaiming 'Why, this is outrageous! You could sue this woman for what she has written.' Thereafter, whether it was the plaque in the Franciscan monastery commemorating the generosity of that great benefactor of Ragusa, the Austrian Count Amerling, or the Imperial Hotel electricity generator – 'the first in Ragusa put in by whom? Miss West's "stupid" Austrians' – I was constantly reminded of the city's debt to the Habsburgs.'You should be reading Thackeray, monsieur. *Henry Esmond*, much more intelligent.'

Beyond the Porta Pile gate, through which Ksenja rarely consented to pass, I was urged by her to explore the narrow streets along the water which, shielded from cafés by the handsome former imperial naval cadet school, are rarely visited by tourists. Here are some of the city's oldest houses. One with a fine oven bulging out into the street dates from well before 1667, the year forever engraved in Ragusan history as the date of the earthquake which all but shattered the city. Three times the sea rose as a wall and dashed the houses of the town to pieces. Hundreds perished that day when St Biagio, the patron saint of the city, whose image appears on the Porta Pile and whose presence saved the city during so many sieges, appears to have deserted the Ragusans in their hour of need. After the devastation each new house, whether visited by the Jesuits or not, received the IHS monogram to ward off any further catastrophe. But here in this picturesque suburb, close to a huge rock released in 1667 from Monte Sergio above the city and which now rests over a small bay below the Fortress of San Lorenzo, the mark of the Jesuit is scarce. Many sons from these houses were however no doubt scholars at the Jesuit Collegium Ragusiensis at the top of the spectacular steps which rise within the old town on the other side of the nearby Porta Pile.

Further out is a remarkable pine-clad avenue carved out of the cliff. A path leads down to a small convent church known for centuries as Chiesa alla Dancé, built in 1457 to provide a resting place after death for the city poor. It has a magnificent renaissance porch carved of Istrian marble. Behind the avenue another half-concealed path runs down to a villa of handsome classical proportions in whose garden are some of the most eccentric archaeological remains in Dalmatia. The villa belonged to a Ragusan naval officer who on his travels discovered a number of curious mementoes. Around his garden, he arranged an odd selection of architectural fragments completely without parallel elsewhere in Europe: grotesques, Etruscan capitals, and grinning dwarves. This is a bizarre excursion into the eccentricities of nineteenth-century archaeology. The pieces are fairly classical in style but with remarkable carvings dating possibly from the sixteenth century, possibly from much earlier. No one in Dubrovnik these days can explain them and even Ksenja, who knew the man who last owned them, was unsure of their provenance. Nor is there much guidance to be had on these puzzling objects in the fine naval museum up on the wall near the Porta Ploca. 'What villa? What objects?' asked a curator, a man who no doubt owed his position to political influence rather than specialised knowledge.

However pleasant the mornings spent exploring Dubrovnik, sooner or later it is time to move on further south, putting this civilised interlude behind one and preparing once more to penetrate the Balkan fastnesses. A few miles south of the city rises Cavtat with another exquisitely ornate church façade and on a small hill the finest creation our old friend Mestrovič ever raised.

The melancholy story of the Račič Mausoleum befits a building which is the summit of Mestrovič's achievement. The Račič family were of old Croatian stock and for centuries were loyal servants of the Habsburgs. At the end of the First World War, Spanish influenza ravaged Dalmatia as it did everywhere else in the Balkans. As the family died one by one, two surviving members decided to erect a small memorial. By the time it was complete, both of these relations had also succumbed to the epidemic; not, however, before they had chosen a site which is one of the most magnificent in the entire Mediterranean. The cypress-covered promontory at Cavtat is the acropolis hill of the ancient Epitaurum; a half-Hellenic, half-Illyrian city, Cavtat rejoiced later in the name of Ragusa Vecchia and thus enjoyed a relationship with Ragusa similar to that of Salona with Spalato.

Like Diocletian's palace in Spalato, the mausoleum is made of white crystalline marble from the island of Brač. The chapel stands out on this lonely promontory in the form of an octagon surrounded by an amphitheatre of towering cliffs that bear down upon it with their massive weight. In general appearance it recalls the tomb of Theodoric at Ravenna. Inside the ceiling of the main chapel is a gable roof decorated with panels about two feet square, some containing inset reliefs of cherubs' heads with folded wings and others pairs of holy doves. These panels are perhaps the most Byzantine of all of Mestrovič's work.

The whole building is a perfect harmony of architecture and sculpture, symbol and fact, of legend and history. Here are contained the records of the Račič family, the story of the local saint, the history of the Crucifixion, the symbolic figure of the Virgin and Child. There is no hint of creed or of any special type of Christianity.

The building is quite simply religious in the most powerful and profound way. Above in a belfry stands a bell which has engraved on it the following legend:

> To know the secret of life you must first know the secret of death.
> To know the secret of death you must first know the secret of love.
> Know the secret of love and you will know the secret of life everlasting.

As Stanley Casson observed in 1928, there is no monument in the world like it and in the early evening light none which enjoys so poignant a setting.

But however calm the sea at the foot of the mausoleum, behind us rises the first spectacular peak of the Black Mountain (Montenegro). Along the winding road south of Cavtat, past the old town of Bar and the vine-draped houses and fortifications of Castelnuovo, birthplace of Trieste's Baron Banfield, lie the tremendous fiords of Kotor, and the great winding road to Lovčen and the capital of Montenegro, Cetinje. 'Mister where you go?' The grey-eyed taxi driver disturbed my wistful thoughts at the foot of the Račič Mausoleum. 'To Crna Gora,' I replied. 'Ha! Crna Gora!' he laughed. 'Crazy place! Every man two metre tall! Every man gun. Why you go mister? Better stay here.'

Certainly nothing looked more inviting than the fish restaurants of Cavtat opening their shutters in the tranquil afternoon light, but the rougher world of the Balkans beckoned, though I was not to know then that I would once again be bumping into Mestrovič in an even more astonishing location.

4 BLACK MOUNTAIN DIPLOMACY

Not for nothing does Kotor enjoy the reputation of the most defensible natural harbour in the Mediterranean. In the days before air-power and the Exocet, a fleet of more than a hundred ships could find shelter in the innermost of that dramatic series of fiords which, protected by shore batteries, was unassailable by the most modern warships. Today it is argued that the tremendous natural advantages of its situation, which persuaded the Austrians in 1916 to move most of their fleet here, no longer carry much weight in an era of nuclear warfare. Perhaps this is true but on more than one occasion in recent years, *perestroika* and *glasnost* notwithstanding, Moscow has asked for permission to station 'some vessels' in Kotor and secure a warm-water port.

Kotor is a quaint little town though its situation at the foot of a tremendous range of mountains accounts for it receiving painfully little sunlight in winter, while in summer the same geographical feature ensures that it is a heat-trap best avoided. The only building of architectural merit is the cathedral; the streets of glorious white stone are the last we will see for some time. With Kotor behind us, we say farewell to Dalmatia and take the famous Lovčen road to an altogether different world.

The advantages of Venice's civilising grace encountered ever since reaching Rab are well behind us. The road we now follow is the finest piece of engineering of its type in Europe, a maze of long zigzags cut into overhanging mountains, for the Lovčen saddle is more than 3,000 feet above us and the precipice in part is a sheer drop. Constructed in the 1840s by the Austrians, it has no fewer than sixty-six zigzags and though the 'new' road constructed in 1906 is gentler, no one wishing to capture the best views of the bay will neglect this older, more dramatic route.

First it passes through a pleasant valley wooded with oaks. At about 3,050 feet above sea level a retrospective view almost unsurpassed in Europe opens up revealing not only a series of great lakes but also to the north-west the Adriatic. Foolishly, the first time I undertook this journey I did so in a car belonging to two reckless Albanians who stopped to give me a lift. It was with that suspect confidence which passes in the Mediterranean lands for bravado that they determined, despite the prominent signs to the contrary, to overtake almost everybody they could see, and several vehicles they could not. To the right the drop to the water was sheer. As if to heighten the sense of drama, the driver insisted on lighting a cigarette at intervals during which he took both hands off the steering wheel. However cool I affected to remain, I more than once vowed never to hitch a lift again. With considerable relief I was deposited at Njegus, a small village in a bleak Karst district and the birthplace of the greatest of all Montenegrin princes, Njegus or Peter II, who ruled from 1830 to 1851. It is to this day an unpretentious place; barely a dozen homes making up the cradle of Montenegrin independence.

It was here that I first set eyes on that legendary sight which made the Montenegrins joke fifty years ago that their most successful export was their sensationally beautiful women. A tall, pale-skinned, dark-haired woman with high cheekbones and a dazzling smile asked me where I was from. In her hand I was surprised to see a copy in French of Thomas More's *Utopia*. Almost at once Baedeker's words came back: 'At places the traveller encounters quite a Homeric state of society, where war and poetry are the sole pursuits and where the hero is seen seated in the presence of the blind minstrel who extols his exploits in war or his last *ceta* or predatory expedition to the twang of the one-stringed *gusla*.' In few passages of Baedeker is the dry Saxon so visibly moved by his surroundings.

'Sladjena', which I was assured means 'sweetie-pie', was not only strikingly good-looking, but her bearing and slender grace conveyed a courtesy which was essentially unspoiled simplicity. Such looks belong to the mountains and are an entirely different variation of that equally absorbing theme of feminine beauty encountered below in the Dalmatian towns. Whether in Tibet or the western highlands of Scotland, I have never ceased to wonder at that quality of grace, *portamento*, which in its simple dignity is a fundamental requisite of beauty and which is so often the preserve of mountain women. Even today when what is known as civilisation has penetrated

48

almost every remote fastness of the Alps and the Carpathians, this unashamedly old-fashioned beauty is still to be found; faces which never betray a trace of grovelling, expressions which are not marred by shuffling meanness. In 1908, Colonel Barry could write of the Montenegrins: 'The whole tone of the national character is bracing. Life in Montenegro is a paltry bauble, only worth a trigger's touch, unless it can be sustained with the purest air of liberty and the proud consciousness of self-respect.'

The handsome Sladjena had studied French at the Sorbonne and returned sporadically as a guide to her native land with groups of tourists. For a few moments – all too short – her charges wandered around the hotel which in 1841 saw the birth of Prince Nicola, Montenegro's first monarch and a man most famous for his daughters, who took the royal courts of Europe by storm, securing between them the Crown Prince of Italy, a Russian grand-duke and a clutch of German *fürsts*. These tales of Montenegrin royalty provoked talk of the Black Mountain, its past and its future. Were the Montenegrins really so different from the Serbs? Yes, came the emphatic reply. 'Different men, different women, but', and here I was given the fastest wink I have ever seen, 'when it suits us we can be Serbs as well.' And with that, her long fingers clutched her book and with a sharp word of command the driver of her bus assembled the perspiring group of French pensioners and I was offered a lift to Cetinje, surely the quaintest former royal capital in Europe. Would my beautiful companion be spending the night in the capital? No, she would much prefer to but the French, ever desirous of material comforts, had long protested at Cetinje's lack of suitable hotels and they would be pressing on to Titograd, the new capital of Montenegro where, though most of the architecture was built in 1970, there existed a passable hotel, by Montenegrin standards.

As we reached the small road which runs for a half mile into Cetinje I felt more than a tinge of regret that Titograd was not on my itinerary as well, but as I jumped off the bus my mind cleared itself of distractions enough to ask Sladjena where I should stay in Cetinje. 'There is no hotel,' came the reply (was there a hint of enthusiasm?). Then perhaps I should go on to Titograd, I ventured, keeping my eye firmly on the straightest nose I had ever seen in the Balkans. 'No, ask for Gospodja Maria. She'll look after you,' came the no doubt well-meant but withering reply. In a cloud of dust the bus drove off.

How often is the mind tortured by the reflection of what might have been after so ephemeral an encounter with a woman of over-whelming attractions? In Graz in the foothills of the Eastern Alps I had often been warned about the dangers of such 'all too frequent possibilities'. Some Austrians had even brought these unrequited encounters down to a fine art. 'Never forget that ultimately the most satisfying relationship with a woman you can ever have is in a café when, seated at opposite ends of the room, your eyes can occasionally meet. You can dream, but say a word and you are doomed,' an old friend had warned. This Central European approach, predictably weak and vacillating, seemed out of place amidst scenery which positively encouraged one to indulge in specu-lations based on fancies which had, frankly, let rip.

With a surprising lightness of tread I set off for Cetinje, indifferent to the extraordinary bleakness of my surroundings and the fact that, though assured I was but a half-hour's march from the city, not a building could be seen. This was not surprising, I later discovered, for as Colonel Barry recalled, the natural heart of Cetinje is a mere hamlet. For the first ten minutes I saw scarcely a sign of life except for the lizards scrambling in the dust. Barren, bleak and grey, the multitudinous peaks evoked a savage grandeur. Not for nothing had the Turk failed over the centuries to penetrate their fastnesses. Time and again an army of Janissaries had wound its way up to Lovčen only to be massacred wholesale by the Mon-tenegrins, whose ferocity sent a chill down the spine of every Turkish general. Before the First World War, the road entering the capital was decorated with a row of skulls, the only visible remains of the last Turkish expedition to attempt to quell these mountain dwellers.

In 1912, an Austrian doctor found to his great surprise that myopia was almost unknown among the Montenegrins. Gen-erations of men and women upon whose sharp eyes behind a rifle sight the lives of families depended have left the Montenegrins still with remarkably powerful vision. During the First World War, however, the fighting qualities of the Montenegrins were less obvi-ously to the fore and an Austrian army of occupation reached Cetinje. Prince Nicola, his eye cast on foreign favours, had played a deep game with his Serbian kinsmen and the Austrians. When by 1916 Belgrade's fate appeared sealed, with Serbia attacked on three fronts, the Prince recalled his troops. On 16 July Lovčen was taken by the Austrians, commanded – it was later pointed out – by an old gambling friend of the Prince's eldest son, the former Austrian military attaché at Cattaro, Colonel Hupka. So intimate was the friendship between the Colonel and the Crown Prince, Peter, that for years afterwards the rumour was widespread that Prince Peter had given the Austrians sandals to help scale the heights more easily. At the same time Prince Nicola asked two of his commanders to refrain from further resistance. In any event the Austrian military cemetery at the foot of Lovčen contains only thirteen graves, soldiers it is said who lost their footing reaching the mountain the Austrians had coveted for years. 'We suspect', wrote the British Minister in Cetinje before his hurried departure from the city, 'that His Majesty is playing a very ambiguous game.'

Such ambiguity was perhaps inevitable after the favours and enormous flattery bestowed upon him by all the major European powers, who almost without exception went out of their way to ingratiate themselves with the monarch of this key strategic position. Around the shanty town of one- and two-storey houses, the grand legations of the great powers paid the Prince a visible compliment. The Russians, whose five-storey legation with two gate-houses still stands out with regal aloofness, were particularly fascinated by Montenegro. The Russian Empress Maria Feodorowna founded in 1869 at her husband's instigation a 'Girls' Institution', an exclusive finishing school outside Cetinje to ensure that all future exports of the princedom were educated to the highest possible standards, learning – as was only right – of the importance of the Russian Tsar's empire and its role as patron state of all Slavs.

Today Cetinje still breathes a spirit of diplomatic intrigue even if the fine legations are now converted into schools and libraries. After a further twenty minutes' tramp I found myself in a large garden of pine trees in one corner of which rose a small five-bay villa upon whose faded stucco façade a metal plate announced 'Her Britannic Majesty's Legation'. The building had seen happier times. Boarded up, a wooden column from its portico lying horizontally in the garden, it was a melancholy sight. No doubt it had since 1916 been used as something other than a legation but coming across it in its present dishevelled state it seemed as if the Minister had only burnt his ciphers the week before. Behind the house, the lawn was still trim, a few spruce firs – imported from Scotland? – providing a pleasant island of shade for what must have been each week the highlight of the Legation wives' social life: the Minister's wife's tea-party. A door left open at the side of the villa revealed the usual post-withdrawal chaos. On the floor of the hall where no doubt many a British traveller to Cetinje was met by Mr R. J. Kennedy, the British Minister resident before the First World War, it was pleasant to find broken but not destroyed the remains of some unmistakably Victorian English encaustic tiles. In another room a few patches of wallpaper were also faintly reminiscent of the gothic revival and the Oxford Movement. In these rather spartan surroundings the gifted and most robust officers of the consular services of great empires vied with each other for the Prince's favour. No doubt dressed up to the nines with the richly gold-embroidered livery of the times, they must have cut quite a dash on their way to the Prince's palace for their weekly audience.

Curiously Mr Kennedy, like most of his predecessors, left no record, apart from his telegrams, of these comic opera occasions. Colonel Barry however has left us with a picture of the 'typical' Montenegrin citizen with whom these ministers must often have dealt. 'The men of Cetinje', he writes, 'are distinguished for the picturesqueness of their wardrobes. No dress in the world is comparable with it for effect. Look at those long jack-boots of supple leather and of graceful fit; the Turkish trousers of a dark shade of Austrian blue; the bolero jacket of an amaranthine cloth, almost a cerise, handsomely embroidered with gold cord and a lavish garniture of smart gold buttons; the round military pill-box cap of the same material edged with black – in historic remembrance of some native sorrow – with the initials of the sovereign on the crown; and then the folds of many-coloured silk coiled round the waist in a voluminous sash to support the ubiquitous leather wallet with its revolver. Every Montenegrin carries a revolver. It is always in his sash and it is invariably loaded.' The prevalence of such picturesque dress meant that the foreigners resident in Cetinje had standards to maintain, however far away from Europe they might feel. Baedeker's terse note, 'Audience with His Highness only in uniform or white tie', refers all too clearly to the very least a self-respecting Englishman could appear in.

From the former British Legation a track through some more pine trees led to what is still Cetinje's main street. No doubt in 1910 this was an imposing mall. Today, flanked by few buildings higher than two storeys, all of which are in a state of advanced dilapidation, it appears peculiarly quaint. So little paint has been applied to the façades since Prince Nicola's day that one can see through the thin peeling stucco on some of the buildings clear signs of the Second World War Italian occupation: 'Osteria', 'Ristorante' – characteristic traces of Italy's brief era of colonial expansion.

The Italian fascist occupation of Cetinje was short-lived – it lasted barely two years – but was not without drama. The Duke D'Aosta, created Prince of Montenegro amidst great flourish in Rome, never overcame his fear of the well-known martial instincts of the inhabitants of the Black Mountain sufficiently to set foot in his new domain. On the first day of the Italian occupation, the order was posted in Serbian and Italian that all weapons were to be handed into the *carabinieri* office by 6 a.m. the following morning. The memory of the days of Prince Nicola when every man carried a revolver was still understandably vivid for the nervous occupying power. But come 6 a.m., the assembled *carabinieri* officers found outside the guardroom only three weapons – all of them rifles 'borrowed' from Italian sentries.

At the end of the mall, a road lined with plane trees leads to the former French Legation which, constructed with that pomp so close to the Frenchman's heart, is a far more imposing establishment than Mr Kennedy's house. A modern suburban villa which would not have looked out of place in the Paris, Vienna or Berlin of the 1920s, it is an opulent essay in Jugendstil, or Art Nouveau as the French would no doubt have insisted on calling it. Today it serves as a well-stocked library, the children's section thereof fully exploiting the mosaic inlay of the panelling to allow each child a charming and colourful niche in which to select his or her reading matter for the long hot afternoons.

Not far from the French Legation was the Italian Residence but this, an equally ambitious villa, was dwarfed by the bright red imperial Russian Legation – the only building in Cetinje to have seen a coat of paint in recent years. Its Italianate windows, suggesting a disturbing mixture of St Petersburg and Florence, appear even more out of place today than they did eighty years ago. Even then one wonders what was the reaction of the Montenegrin royal family to the construction of a building larger than either of Prince Nicola's two palaces by a no means unequivocally friendly power.

The Prince's engaging palaces, both two storeys high and built in the classical style, are a little way to the west. In the most important of these, the so-called Billiard Palace, there is a museum devoted to the Prince's family. Among the portraits and books of poetry – Prince Nicola was a playwright of some note, his *Empress of the Balkans* receiving rave reviews in Belgrade – there are some English military decorations. These it would seem date from the Crimean War and were bestowed on Turkish officers who fought alongside the Coldstream Guards at that spectacular feat of British arms, the Battle of the Alma. Later the same Turkish officers fell while fighting against the Montenegrins who, after severing their foes' heads from their bodies in the time-honoured tradition of the homeland, no doubt presented their prince with these trophies of war.

Such nineteenth-century glamour was by no means remote on my last visit to the palace. In October 1989, to the obvious delight of all Montenegrins, their monarch's remains returned for reburial. The Prince had fled to Paris in 1916 and eventually died in Italy. The return of Nicola's remains not only followed tremendously complicated negotiations with the Italian government but also, more significantly, occurred at a time when growing nationalism throughout the country was threatening to dissolve the entire federation.

These black clouds on the horizon were however forgotten that sunny and warm October of 1989, when Cetinje indulged in non-stop celebration for more than twenty-four hours. Every shop, every café and restaurant was in action throughout the night. Most spectacular of all, however, were the arrangements around the royal palace. This proud if modest building with its fine white portico was also permanently open, but only the production of an old engraved *Times* card was able to secure admission to wander alone through candlelit rooms which appeared unchanged since the late monarch's unfortunate and hasty flight. While a guided tour painstakingly examined the uniforms below I discovered upstairs a magnificent bedroom with dark green wallpaper and black furniture. In one corner a portrait of Queen Victoria looked frostily on while in another a photograph of a family signed in a neat but indecipherable hand suggested a farewell present from a British minister.

In the dim light, this room appeared eminently practical and habitable – closer to a cosy late Victorian villa in Bedford Park than a country house. The larger and better-lit salons were, however, not unimpressive. In one decorated with paintings of Vesuvius a long polished mahogany table was laid as if at any moment the Prince, escorted by numerous *aides de camp* in full dress, might come strutting in and sit down for a full-scale banquet.

A few yards away in the former Bulgarian Legation, now a reputable café with a fine 1930s panelled interior, it was early morning but still cards were being shuffled at all the corner tables. At one of these a few young Montenegrins read poetry aloud while another strummed the one-stringed *gusla*, producing an eerie noise which penetrated the dawn air. Half a mile from here in the new and startlingly ugly Hotel Grand the heir to the throne was holding informal court in a basement restaurant. The Prince, also confusingly called Nichola, an architect from Paris, found the simplest Serbo-Croat phrase a trial but was served with enthusiasm by the staff of the hotel. A benign-looking man with a monastic haircut, he was accompanied by a beautiful and sultry wife who appeared as bemused as he by the warmth of their reception by the Montenegrins. In one hand she carried like a talisman an old cigarette case with the Montenegrin eagle engraved on the lid, while in true Erich von Stroheim style she puffed on a cigarette in a long black holder.

All around them were representatives of distinguished Balkan families. In one corner stood about twenty octogenarian Italians, all dressed in sombre black suits and all wearing the same tie and equipped with armbands displaying the cypher of the House of Savoy. In another lounged a group of Austrian aristocrats, immediately recognisable by their noisy accents and unbelievably tactless habit of barging up to the Prince every five minutes with requests for an autograph. Moving from one group to another came a cigarette seller stocked with a special version of John Player's First World War cigarettes illustrating the 'Allied War Hero no. 28 HM King of Montenegro'.

It became apparent that if the Montenegrin government was sincerely keen on replenishing its empty reserves of hard currency it could do no better than stage a ball every autumn, charging £100 a ticket, and keep the city celebrating for twenty-four hours in contemporary costume. A Montenegrin carnival would I suspect outsell anything Venice has to offer these days, providing a combination of picturesque fancy dress and exotic location, low prices and a deeply hospitable local populace. But on my first visit to the capital, such reflections were far in the future. In a café next to the main square, a cup of Turkish coffee prepared one for the challenge of finding Gospodja Maria. The cafés in Cetinje, as elsewhere in Montenegro and, to a lesser extent, in Bosnia, are the preserve of the menfolk. Whatever the social consequences of two world wars, a *coup d'état* and four decades of communism, nothing has changed in Cetinje *vis à vis* the rights of the fairer sex. Where the beautiful Amazons of Cetinje were I could not tell, but their husbands and their sons were clearly all in the cafés, hour after hour, day after day, week after week, languidly smoking cigarettes from long wooden holders, playing cards or just quietly watching the world go by over a glass of powerful rakir, the ubiquitous locally-brewed spirit.

Had any of these gentlemen an idea of Gospodja Maria's whereabouts? A wizened, dreamy man placing his cards down on a next-door table with a resounding smack gave me a look which fifty years ago I imagined would have decided my fate in a second. 'Try the tourist office'; another card smacked down on the table. It was dusk by the time I located this, but a dark-skinned lady sat smiling behind the desk. '*Dobro Govorite Srbski*' – 'You speak good *Srbski*.' What I thought were words of Croat or at least Serbo-Croat from this point onwards were always described as '*Srbski*'. Gospodja Maria? Just across the road above the chemist's, came the obliging reply.

The chemist's was a splendid relic of the nineteenth century with glass bottles, varnished shelves and a white statue of Aphrodite in the window. Next to this a narrow flight of wooden stairs led up to a door of ancient wood. After a few knocks Gospodja Maria appeared, a lady of about fifty with a strong Italianate face wearing a dressing-gown of oriental silk. Her rooms were festooned with garish hand-coloured 1930s views of the Italian lakes – another memento of the war? Through a small door which looked like a cupboard more steps led up to the attic, where a small room furnished with two long Biedermeier beds had been constructed many years ago. Through the two small skylights, the view as far as the eye could see was just jagged rock. 'You will sleep well here,' she said, and despite the barking of wolves echoing noisily about the mountains, I did.

Wherever one stands in Cetinje, it is impossible not to see on looking up the vast peak of the Lovčen. The top appeared however to be flattened slightly and on asking Gospodja Maria over coffee and some delicious hot rolls the following morning about the mountain she told me that on the summit was the mausoleum of the great Prince Njegus, poet-soldier and statesman, the founder of the new era in Montenegrin history and the prince who more than anyone established the Homeric tradition of Montenegrin life. But how to get there? Was there a bus? No, said Gospodja Maria. Taxi? Very expensive, sighed Gospodja Maria. Well, I would walk. 'Twenty miles, *Gospodin*,' came the reply; but we both agreed that it was more than likely that I should be able to cadge a lift on the way.

The road to the great Lovčen heights runs past the last of the legations, the Austrian, also an imposing building though with less swagger than the Russian one. It was curious to see the chapel, a fine structure as one might expect of a power whose emperors were not only All Highest but also Apostolic, stuffed as far up as the clerestory windows with bits of furniture. The rest of the Legation ironically enough is now the headquarters of the Cetinje police force. Beyond this building the road begins to climb in slow curves. After the fifth of these to my disappointment my lift, acquired in a café near the town centre, halted, saying he had gone as far as he intended to that day, and would I care for a glass of rakir from his home on the next corner? It was the only house to be seen, bar a few farms up on the hills. Above towered the great wall of rock on which rose what appeared from below to be a giant grey coffin.

It was past noon by the time I managed to divest myself of Montenegrin hospitality and I began to walk quickly, occasionally looking back in the hope of seeing a vehicle. The desolation of the area was powerful even in the bright sunlight; footsteps echoed into the distant hills; large ravens circled overhead. The road in fact only dated from the late 1960s, before which a far more tortuous path stretched up to the remains of Prince Njegus. Until the First World

War, these had been sheltered from the elements, which at 6,000 feet above sea level are considerable, by a modest chapel. Then in 1915 what the thunder and lightning of this most stormy part of the country failed to do was accomplished by the formidable Austrian 30.5 cm Skoda howitzers and the chapel was destroyed.

In the 1960s the communists, rather than reconstruct this small chapel, decided to give life to a plan originally drawn up by Mestrovič in the 1930s to rehouse the remains in an altogether more dramatic mausoleum. Few issues were as hotly contested at the time in the Jugoslav press and the plan was opposed by historians and artists throughout the country who claimed the colossal marble and granite figures of the Mestrovič scheme would entirely destroy the mountain's peak. The road I was trudging along therefore had been built less for the use of pilgrims than to ensure that the vast marble figures, which if not hewn by the master himself had nonetheless been designed by him, made their way up to the storm-prone mountain as easily as possible.

By the time a friendly Bosnian doctor who drove past an hour and a half later deposited me at the summit it was difficult not to agree with Mestrovič's detractors. The figures are vast – perhaps six times life size – and after the simple modesty of the Račič family chapel they come as something of a shock, for they are so clearly not hewn by the same hand. Those who knew this summit before 1971 would miss the simplicity of what was there then and which, given the character of Prince Njegus, must be considered more appropriate. But on the roof of the Balkans with the snow-capped peaks stretching away in all directions the sheer exhilaration of the view blinds even the most critical eye to the failings of this monument.

One reaches the tomb by descending dark steps, where one is overwhelmed by a vast figure depicting the Prince in contemplative mood. By the time the mausoleum was completed Mestrovič had been dead many years and I cannot help wondering whether that master, who knew the simple traditions of the Montenegrins so well, would on reflection have still been in favour of this monumental early project. But there can be no doubt that the large caryatids illustrating the Montenegrin woman on the exterior of the mausoleum come into their own when a storm breaks about the Lovčen peaks, as it generally does each evening in the summer.

Almost imperceptibly a cloud 'no bigger than a man's hand' appeared in the east; then another and then another. Within an hour the sky had turned a metallic grey; twenty minutes later it was virtually black. The apocalyptic nature of these electrical storms epitomises Burke's ideal of the sublime: 'The passion caused by the great and sublime in nature is astonishment; and astonishment is that state of the soul in which all its emotions are suspended with some degree of horror.'

Terror would however have been closer to my reaction. The lightning illuminated the caryatids in a most grotesque fashion. If Njegus had not been such a benign figure in Montenegrin history I believe there would have been grounds for serious unease. But like most storms in the Balkans this one if noisy died out within another hour, though not before my nerves had been tested to the limit. There is no more exposed situation in the country than that of Mount Lovčen, and as the thunder rolled with a deafening crescendo above and around us, the curator of the museum bade me descend into the vault. It would be safer. There are, of course, lightning conductors he assured me, 'but you never know.' Perched at the edge of a giant toe, the realisation of Mestrovič's most monolithic creation, I regarded in the flickering light the enormous foot of the poet-prince. As I did so the words uttered at Cavtat less than forty-eight hours before came back to taunt me: 'Crna Gora. Crazy place.'

5 THE SANJAK OF NOVI BAZAR

Three days later and thunder was still echoing round the Montenegrin mountains. As a cloudburst soaked those unlucky enough to be without a hat or umbrella on the wide streets of Titograd, I glanced at my watch. It was high summer and only 7.30 p.m. but the sky was black. Rashly perhaps I had decided to attempt to reach Sarajevo and Bosnia by rail rather than by what was presumably a more arduous route across country. An 'express' was due at eight o'clock but little did I know then of the vagaries of Titograd railway station, surely the most unattractive place to be found anywhere in the Balkans.

Before the war Podgorica, as this town was then called, consisted of little more than a few streets and a mosque. Both the Italians and the Germans found it, however, quite useful as a defensible airfield for raiding operations against the partisans. It was then, I imagine, even at the height of occupation a more agreeable place than it is today. Long faceless streets of flats, all uniformly drab and all dating, as far as an inexperienced eye could tell, from the early years of the '70s, do not encourage one to linger.

Rising up in the centre of this concentration of remorseless concrete to deliver the *coup de grâce* to the senses is probably the dirtiest and ugliest railway station in Europe. A flash of lightning appeared to strike a lamppost just outside it as I approached and for a moment I thought I might be witnessing an overdue moment of retribution but no, the lamppost spluttered and spun round but did not crash on to any of the platforms.

Inside the station all was confusion. A tall, blonde English girl, with that familiar combination of dreaminess and hardness, returned from the lavatories exclaiming loudly in the blue-chip tones of Sloane Square that even Calcutta was cleaner. Along three platforms well under cover the Jugoslav army, forever it seems spending every moment of its spare time in a railway station, dug in for a long night and produced sleeping bags. 'The train is late,'

61

philosophised a harassed station master, his red cap soaked by rain to a dull shade of rust. There was no indication as to how late but after an hour most of the civilians had decamped to the smoke-filled *kavana* which, doing a brisk trade in beer, was now the only dry place left in the station not exclusively given over to snoring soldiery.

It was eleven o'clock and still pouring with rain before the train, a brown and yellow electric affair, arrived, clanking ominously before screeching to a halt in front of the buffers. What followed was the closest two human masses can ever be to hand-to-hand fighting without actually coming to serious blows. As if the manœuvre was a long-practised tactic of the modern Jugoslav army, the soldiers suddenly rose up *en masse* and rushed to the doors of each carriage, skirmishing wildly as they pushed their luggage and in some cases themselves through the windows. Whether this strategy would have succeeded even with an empty train is questionable. No doubt the traditions of partisan warfare develop precisely that lithe, flexible and above all forceful propulsion of the body now in evidence but it was clear by the cries and oaths, taken together both loud enough to drown the thunder above, that such a tactic of warfare did not make allowances for any organised resistance.

Titograd is the end of the line. Titograd Central is therefore a terminus from which no one can hope to depart except back in the direction whence they came. This was clear to most of us gazing across the platform from the bar, and was equally clear to every passenger on the incoming train. But to the battalion which rose up to contest every inch of carriage space this simple truth was either invisible or irrelevant. And as is frequently the case in the Balkans, despite the overwhelming odds fortune favoured the defenders who closed ranks, thereby preventing more than a handful of the military from entering the train in the first charge.

Where such tremendous scenes of human endeavour would have ended could not be hazarded. In the event a third party intervened to halt play. For stealing in to the neighbouring platform, almost unseen and unheard, came another train with carriages boldly marked 'Sarajevo'. First perceived as a feint, suspicion turned rapidly to conviction as the troops realised that they had in fact been storming the wrong objective. By that time I'm glad to say most of the civilians, myself included, had bagged at least some standing room so that the shock of the army's arrival could be withstood with some calm. In the event, though this train too was vigorously occupied, the teeth of the troops had been drawn; much energy had it seemed been expended in the first mêlée and the men were more subdued. It was still raining at five minutes past midnight when the train, loaded to bursting point, made its way up the mountains towards Novi Bazar and the Sanjak. In the darkness it was impossible to appreciate the scenery though from time to time a flash of lightning illuminated as dramatic a vista as any encountered in Montenegro.

The area the train was heading for is perhaps the most romantic part of the Balkans. But look at a map of Jugoslavia for the Sanjak of Novi Bazar and apart from a small town marked N. Bazar, there is no indication that this is a region in any way different from the rest of Serbia. Under complete Turkish rule until 1878, the Sanjak consisted entirely of a rough defile in the mountain belt separating Montenegro from Serbia. Its people were mostly Serbian, but Islam-icised Serbs, not Christians. Albanians and Turks also lived in the Sanjak which, though garrisoned by the Austrians after 1878, reverted in 1908 to Turkish administration as a quid pro quo for Austria's annexation of Bosnia and Herzegovina. As such it was therefore the declining Turkish Empire's westernmost salient in the Balkans, a bastion of Islam in a state of considerable chaos and some violence.

In August 1912 Aubrey Herbert, that distinguished Balkan traveller who was later offered the crown of Albania and who was the model for the hero of John Buchan's *Greenmantle*, found the Sanjak 'a no-man's land occupied by the Turks, held precariously by the Albanians, ruled by none'. An Austrian consul advised him: 'Do not go to Sanjak; it's a desperate place since we left it.' Today, such danger is remote though I should have given much to see our train attacked and liberated from its army occupation. As we gathered gathered speed and left the Montenegrin frontier behind, it was painful to have to resign myself to spending the next six hours standing in a cramped space at the end of a carriage opposite a foul-smelling lavatory whose door, swinging to and fro, would not remain shut. It was not the first time I had travelled in such conditions and a few square inches of window allowed an occasional glimpse of the lightning-lit mountains. But at Prijepolje tolerance was pushed to its utmost limits by the arrival of three women with a clearly liverish child whose incessant screaming would have unhinged the most placid of temperaments. It was past one o'clock in the morning but I was determined to leave the train at the next station and if necessary sleep in a bus shelter rather than put up with this din for much longer. The storm was abating and nowhere could be less comfortable than this stuffy tin on wheels.

Within five minutes of this resolution the train stopped. Had it come to a halt a little later when things had quietened down I might well have had second thoughts; human nature is so fickle in adversity. I managed to open the door just as the train began to move off again. Outside there was no platform, no station, just trees. To the left though were a few lights and behind them what seemed the beginning of a street. The train gathered momentum and I jumped out, relieved to breathe the cool fresh night air.

Five minutes later I was walking along the deserted street of the village of Priboj; shuttered windows and in the distance the tall silhouette of a mosque. Baedeker, surprisingly, for the village appeared literally to be in the midst of nowhere, knew all about the place. In 1905 its population had only numbered 963 souls though the Austrian military station had offered 'acceptable accommodation'. The place was then only accessible by a 'narrow bridle-path' skirting the left bank of a small river flowing through the 'narrow and highly picturesque valley between lofty wooded mountains'. Had it developed at all? In the darkness it seemed not. Of accommodation I could see no sign. A modern and apparently comfortable if uninspiring hotel does exist near the station, I later found out, but in the early hours of the morning this must have been well locked up along with every other dwelling in the village. Walking along, I was glad that the rain had turned to a faint drizzle, but, not surprisingly, there was exceptionally little sign of life. Few of the houses were more than one or two storeys high. Most appeared to have been constructed about the time of the Austrian occupation, with small pieces of Italianate detail about the windows and doors.

Suddenly at a small crossroads the door of one building swung open to reveal a warm red glow, as if a furnace was burning within. So appealing was this in the dark night that I instinctively moved towards it, almost colliding with a shadowy figure also moving towards the source of the light. '*Dobro Vecer* (Good evening),' I ventured. '*Dobro Vecer*,' he replied sympathetically. He was a small man with a dark skin and the round face typical of the western Balkans. He had neither high cheekbones nor a long nose, and his eyebrows were black. He could not have been much more than forty-five though he carried himself with the seriousness of a much older man; his eyes were large, dark and friendly, and following his gaze I saw that what I had first imagined was a fireplace was in fact a large oven beneath a chimney breast. The man was the baker of Priboj. 'I have just been away for two weeks holiday,' he explained in Serbo-Croat. 'Now I am back I must work all night for tomorrow the people of the village will expect much bread.'

To my enquiries after a hotel, he shook his head but then after a few seconds' thought said, 'If you wish, you may have my bed upstairs for tonight I shall not be sleeping.' His face betrayed no sign of subterfuge and his hospitality was so genuine and so welcome that I followed him up a set of rickety steps past more garish prints of the ubiquitous Italian lakes.

The small door at the top creaked open to reveal a large room with two windows, a small but clean bed, several empty bottles, a painted cupboard and yet more pictures of the Italian lakes. In one corner hung a fine parchment which insisted that the bearer had the right to practise the art of bakery and was a 'Master' (second class). The script was certainly not in Cyrillic and a closer examination revealed my host to be an Albanian though there was no sign anywhere of the white fez or *plish* which I understood was an inseparable item of dress for the *squiptu* (Albanian). A modest but clean bathroom was pointed out across a corridor and, mumbling my thanks as best I could, I fell asleep almost as soon as I sat down.

The next morning I awoke to find the sun streaming in through the window and a delicious if powerful smell of baked bread. Outside, in the daylight, Priboj revealed itself to be little more than it had appeared at night: a single mall of Balkan houses with a few side-streets leading towards distant woods. Below the window about a dozen people stood in a line for a loaf of bread. Everywhere one looked, up and down the street, was the same sight of peasant women wearing headscarves of a sombre black bombazine marching along with a golden loaf under one arm. Downstairs trade was brisk; the magnificent fire which had led me here in the first place was extinguished, but piled high like an edible stockade stood the results of a hard night's labour. The baker, unshaven but otherwise looking remarkably awake, was guiding two assistants, young girls in white coats, who were dispatching the loaves as quickly as they could.

As I proffered a note it was quickly indicated that payment for my rest was out of the question, but I was allowed to buy a loaf which at least in my host's eyes was more than adequate reward. This was hospitality indeed for the bread was as excellent as anything I have tasted in Paris and cost the equivalent of threepence.

Such generosity is by no means unusual in the valleys of the former Sanjak, as I found out after bidding the baker farewell and trudging up a street until I found a café. Unlike most cafés in southern Jugoslavia and all those in Montenegro which I had come across, this establishment did not believe in coffee-stained linen. Immaculate white tablecloths met the eye wherever it wandered. As I pulled up a chair, a handsome youth who could barely have been more than fifteen strode out, and with a gesture of clearly Islamic elegance asked what he could offer the *Gospodin*.

He was tall and wiry with very dark skin, high cheekbones and a beautiful profile. He might have been Turkish and yet the face showed clear Slav traits, but if this was my first encounter with an Islamicised Serb I could only marvel at the ripeness of the mix. Here was the strength and dignity of the Slav with the silence and almost intuitive understanding of a guest's needs which is usually associated with the Orient.

I ordered coffee. There arrived, however, as well as the most delicious Turkish coffee I had tasted since Trieste, half a litre of local spring water, slightly fizzy but very cool, and a plate of ripe tomatoes, lettuce and spring onions. As a coda to this uncalled-for munificence, and despite it being only 8.30 a.m., there came a small glass of cognac.

Again I offered to pay but this met with a look of such injury that I hastily returned the note to my wallet. As I tucked into the salad, the patron of the establishment came out, an old but also fine-featured man who was the father of my very generous waiter. We talked of Jugoslavia and he wisely took the long-term view of a true son of a province which had already seen four different masters come and go this century. Looking skywards at the prospect of the future, he said, 'Jugoslavia a good country? Who knows?'

An hour later I was ready to go to catch a bus to Novi Bazar but the arrival of some other Turkish-looking gentlemen, complete with fezes and pantaloons held me up. 'Had I eaten?' 'I must eat more! I am too thin!' This is how I missed the first bus for Novi Bazar. There is something in the southern Slav temperament which makes it exceptionally difficult, once amicable relations have been established, to tell any stranger bad news. It is a weakness by no means limited to the Balkans but it is there that it is encountered at its most frequent. Thus the conversation inevitably went as follows: 'Are there many buses going to Novi Bazar?' 'Of course, many many buses. Novi Bazar is a very fine town.' In fact there are only two and had I not downed my cognac *prestissimo* I should have been stranded in Priboj for another day – agreeably it must be said, for nowhere in the Balkans is as hospitable as the Sanjak.

Given the vagaries of travelling by train in Jugoslavia, there can be no doubt that the buses offer, by comparison, a five-star service. They are faster, more reliable, invariably cleaner and above all regular, operating an impressive network which links the most remote village with virtually every city of note in the country. Pit-stops are frequent, usually at a hostelry selling a combination of reasonable coffee and vile liquor, but as these rarely last longer than fifteen minutes the journey is still accomplished in a fraction of the time it would take by train. By late lunchtime, with the sun still gloriously high, we reached Novi Bazar.

That the town was once of some importance is clear. It was by far the most Turkish in appearance of the places I had seen: minarets everywhere; old wooden (or sometimes wattle and daub) houses; and nearly every woman wearing if not a veil then at least the long synthetic pantaloons which are the modern form of ethnic costume throughout Islamic regions. Along the main street there were several shops and many cafés but the atmosphere differed from that of Priboj: there was more noise, more sullenness and it must be said more laziness. The gestures of the waiters, their looks and their demeanour were less favourable, and having seen and forsaken an idyll I only had myself to blame if the by now unaccustomed tradition of paying for food and drink prevailed, along with a degree of abruptness so remote from the last twenty-four hours that I had forgotten how in the Balkans it was in fact the norm.

Much of the architecture was so picturesque and oriental in aspect that it was difficult to recall the bleakness of Titograd the evening before. But a few miles' walk from the centre of town its character changes. The mountains tower round a small hill on which stands the remarkable church of St Peter in Ras. The building dates largely from the tenth century and it was here that in the twelfth century a council of bishops decided to expel that most curious of all sects in the Balkans, the Bogomils.

The Bogomil heresy remains one of the most disturbing and yet absorbing religious phenomena of Europe. Its tenets are chiefly known from the writings of its enemies who accuse the Bogomils of every imaginable crime. Their creed it seems was strongly influenced by earlier Manichaeism and was based upon dualism, that is the co-existence of a spiritual universe and a world of matter created by Satan. They both rejected the sacraments and despised images. It was a Slav creed, originating in Bulgaria, and popular with those striving to retain some identity in the face of waves of Catholicism and the Orthodox Church.

Persecuted mercilessly by Christians, both Catholics and Orthodox, most of the Bogomils preferred the contemptuous tolerance of the Turks who regarded their Satanic beliefs (in particular that article laying down that only by doing evil could one improve oneself) with the detached air of those for whom all other faiths are equally pagan. Large numbers of Bogomils, however, particularly from the land-owning class, became Muslims in order to retain their property. It was the descendants of these Islamicised Slavs who had been so hospitable towards me in Priboj.

As well as St Peter in Ras, there are other monuments of the twelfth century nearby. The ruined church of St George is the resting place of King Dragutin, the thirteenth-century Serb who fought so hard to keep this part of the country Christian. Despite being used as an observation post by Austrian artillery three times between 1878 and 1916, what remains is not without grace, dignity and atmosphere. Below stretched the village of old Ras, sometimes called Pazarič, with its houses of baked mud and beams. The oriental element prevailed and fuelled a determination to reach the heart of Sarajevo.

From Novi Bazar to Bosnia I was advised first to reach Raška at the edge of the Sanjak, where a bus would take me north through a strip of Serbia and then down to Sarajevo. There is no country in Europe in which it is easier to be side-tracked than modern Jugoslavia. At Raška, an impoverished settlement on the railway, it was market day and a number of fine wizened old men wearing breeches of dark grey wool were huddled together over stalls selling fruit, goats' cheese and vegetables. The Muslim element was no longer so evident and instead of colourful pantaloons, most of the womenfolk of Raška had resorted to that international uniform of the casual classes, blue denims. An exception to these – and it must be said a most welcome one – was the appearance on the other side of the small stream outside the town of a score of Jugoslav girls of about eighteen all dressed in the rather chic khaki uniform of the Jugoslav National Army.

On a small hill rose a three-storey stucco building which appeared to have been converted into a barracks in the late years of the last century. Surrounded by barbed wire and with a dilapidated sentry box at the gates it still served as some military institution. The girls, wide-eyed and laughing, linking arms in a most unsoldierly way, advanced towards the market to be followed by another large group, this time mostly blonde, who with breeches, riding boots and buttoned-up tunics cut a decidedly more military dash, perhaps because they were slightly older. The building from which they all emerged was in fact Serbia's principal academy for young female officers and, while none of the girls I saw were armed with more than a clasp-knife, in the event of hostilities entire legions of Serbian and other Slav women would be formed to be led by these girls, well-versed, it was said, in the art of merciless guerilla warfare.

I found this a little difficult to imagine. The Jugoslav army sets little store by drill and spit and polish and a professional soldier would, I think, have found little to suggest that these girls were anything more than Girl Guides out for a picnic. Their boots were dirty; their tunics, given the generous proportions with which most South Slav women are endowed, were almost bursting; and, perhaps most telling of all, their long fingers were almost entirely decorated with garish pink nail varnish. But then appearances are deceptive and during the war Marshal Tito certainly made use of several striking women 'partisans' who, whatever their actions against the enemy, made a considerable impression on any English liaison officer parachuted into his battle zone. One of these Amazonian *aides de camp* indeed so impressed Churchill in Rome that he insisted on giving her his cigar lighter as a token of his esteem.

The train from Raška was again full of soldiery – was there a war on? This time young boy officer cadets with cropped hair and long cigarette holders took up all of the first-class carriage to Sarajevo. None of them could have been more than seventeen but already they had a quality of earnestness far beyond their years. Long, thin beaky noses; again the old-fashioned high collar and Sam Brown belts all recreated the imagery of *Arms and the Man*. Here were the 'wretched Servians with their dandified officers'. Though rather more care had been taken to keep the coats and hats in immaculate order, their boots remained as grimy as those of their female counterparts, but then in Bosnia no man is judged by the shine of his boots.

6 YOUNG BOSNIA

It is a curious fact that those places which enjoyed brief colonial rule often exude more powerfully the atmosphere of their erstwhile colonial rulers than those places which lived under a foreign flag for centuries. Sarajevo along with the rest of Bosnia-Herzegovina was governed from Vienna for less than forty years and yet there is an astonishing amount even today which is undeniably Austrian.

Unfortunately, this does not apply to the railway station. Whatever opprobrium can be hurled at the Habsburgs, there can be no doubt that the empire could never be criticised for the quality of its railway stations. These splendid neo-Italianate buildings with their peeling yellow stucco and sombre frescoed women gazing down within can be found as far east as Przemysl and Lemberg but not as far south as Sarajevo. 'Progress' has obliterated such relics here and the traveller arrives at a grim concrete establishment with no sign of a cornice but inevitably bristling with soldiery. From here it is a brief tram ride past a very Austrian-looking neo-classical museum and Arts and Crafts tobacco factory to the centre of town which at first sight looks like a more colourful version of Graz.

It is often said that in 1908, when Austria formally annexed the provinces she had occupied since 1878, the chancelleries of Europe were both astonished and horrified. How this could be the case when even the dimmest diplomat could see how the Austrians had spent the last thirty years making Sarajevo as close to Vienna in appearance as possible, is a matter for speculation. Was Europe really so civilised then that it expected Austria, which had lost men, spent millions of crowns and invested more than thirty years in dragging a backward eastward province into the twentieth century, to continue simply to rent the region? Had the Austrians pulled out in 1908, the contrast between western and oriental architecture at least would have been striking. Today, as in 1908, the centre of the town boasts all the sugary vocabulary of architects busy elsewhere in the empire. A typically uninspired if well-made neo-gothic Roman

Catholic cathedral, street after street of light neo-Italianate housing and most memorable of all, overlooking the central square which faces the river, a pale blue façade with those *femme-fatale* Jugendstil faces which to this day appear to breathe languidly the spirit of Klimt and the Vienna Secession. Like cricket architecture can, however, only express the values of the society which supports it. Behind these stucco façades was a bureaucracy laying down rules and codes, and building schools which, however alien to the existing modest infrastructure, have stood the test of time, meriting favourable comparison with nearly everything that has since replaced it.

Of course, as always with the Austrians, there were excesses of taste. The neo-Moorish town hall though quaint today is an unfortunate illustration of the baleful effects an oriental climate can exert on a riotous northern imagination. But museums, cathedrals and opera houses rise on all sides to keep this extravagance in check and to remind the visitor that Mitteleuropa in its heyday bestowed some of its finest virtues on Bosnia. Suddenly however, and without warning, this townscape vanishes. The stucco disappears, even the magnificent red marble paving stones locally quarried and reminiscent of Salzburg peter out and before one has taken more than a dozen steps, the great oriental bazaar closes in on all sides.

The Baščačija with its small wooden stalls, wattle and daub houses and the minarets of a dozen mosques, however tawdry and unexciting, is the Orient *in excelsis*. Even without the curious experience of stepping within a few seconds from early twentieth-century Mitteleuropa into late nineteenth-century Balkania, the sight is highly picturesque. On the left is the Café Jasmin. On autumn mornings the bright sun filters through the modern wooden shutters and cuts shafts of light through the smoke-filled rooms. There are no comfortable chairs in these cafés and one looks in vain for conversation, but here with the incessant wailing of cacophanous music played by Bazouki bands droning on hour after hour, the senses are calmed more speedily than by any sedative. Here as elsewhere in Bosnia the concept of time is totally different to that which is measured by our northern minds. I have spent more than two hours in such a smoke-filled café and felt neither boredom nor restlessness, indeed even without a book or pen and paper it has seemed like no more than fifteen minutes.

Opposite, behind the row of stalls at a small crossroads there

stands the first of the many hat shops in the bazaar. Throughout
the Balkans, indeed throughout Eastern Europe, those whose trade
it is to adorn or protect the head are among the most courteous
people one could hope to meet. In Sarajevo, despite the tourism
which renders the place so cramped in the summer, the hat maker
remains a gentleman. In this particular shop Mustapha, a middle-
aged well-built man with grey hair, after attempting to sell me a
variety of Turkish, Serbian and Albanian headgear settled down
contentedly to discourse on higher things:

'Are you a Catholic?'

'Yes.'

'All Catholic. English Catholic? Very strange and nice but you
must realise there is only one Allah.'

'One Allah?'

'Yes, one Allah.' His eyes opened wide and an orange-peel grin
appeared.

'No priests, no bishops, no pope. Just me and Allah.'

'Direcna Linea?' I ventured in broken Serbo-Croat.

'Direcna Linea!' he answered with that astonishing clarity of
pronunciation which I had first noticed in Montenegro but which
throughout my travels in the Serbian-speaking lands suggested
the vocative and a tradition of hurling oral messages across long
distances in times of foul weather.

Mustapha would, I felt, have spent many an hour longer estab-
lishing the virtues of Islam but hunger forbade further discussion.
'Where', I asked simply, 'could I eat the best Čevapčiči in Bosnia?'
'The best Čevapčiči in Bosnia? You mean the best in all Jugoslavia.
Why here!' came the answer, delivered with the certainty of those
for whom life holds few ambiguities. There are many who will spend
hours in the narrow streets around the celebrated Hubrej Beg
mosque and never come upon the magnificent Čevapi Baščačija, to
which every stall in Jugoslavia selling meat balls must pay homage.
Here, too, the music is loud and wonderfully mindless and the
western visitor though conspicuous will be treated as an equal and
without undue fuss. Onions, Bosnian bread, salt and a free glass of
water accompany this rich and spicy meal which fortifies the body
for that most demanding of tasks, the pursuit of a room. Encouraged by my good fortune in the Sanjak I suggested to the owner of
the Čevapi that it might not be too difficult to find a private room

in Sarajevo. Something quiet, picturesque and friendly? 'Private room, *Gospodin*?', the old man wiped his brow with two pieces of tissue paper usually reserved as napkins for his customers. 'Very difficult in Sarajevo. Old women very cruel.' Then with an intake of breath as he fixed me in the eye, 'Jews, *Gospodin*! Old women Jews! No good private rooms. Expensive.'

He was referring to that curious strand of Sarajevo life which makes it so very much a melting pot of different cultures, its ancient Jewish community. As in Salonica, Spanish-speaking Jews have long been part of the city's population. Wherever the Osmanli have been the Spanish Jew has generally remained. High-cheekboned, dark-coloured and with socket eyes and a thin *retroussé* nose they are the descendants of those who fled from Spain during the time of Isabella, the folk of whom Disraeli more than once wrote with ardour and who gleam in the encounters of Borrow. Some hid their religion and remained in Spain. Others preserved their rites but also sought to carry Spain with them, clinging so faithfully to the tongue of their land that today, four centuries after the event, these Jews still speak Spanish, a Cervantine Spanish, corrupted somewhat by Serbian, Turkish and, possibly, Yiddish additions. Perhaps one is rating the love of Spain too highly in these people. A *lingua secreta*, and Spanish would have served admirably as such in the Balkans, would have been an invaluable aid in all transactions demanding subtlety and discretion.

Although the Sarajevo Jews had suffered greatly at the hands of the Germans during the war, sufficient numbers remained to be viewed with some anti-Semitic feeling by many of the Bosnians to whom I spoke. Though I never found any justification for their accusations of a Jewish monopoly in the private accommodation of the city, it was no doubt the case that private rooms were expensive and unsatisfactory both in location and in condition.

More engaging, though in a state of dilapidation which suggests that progress is particularly slow in this part of the Balkans, is the Hotel Europa. Built by the Austrians in a neo-Italianate style, it is conveniently situated at the centre of the town near the river. As such it is infinitely preferable to the modern skyscraper establishments built miles away from anywhere to house the Winter Olympic enthusiasts who descended on Sarajevo a few years ago bringing, no doubt, much sorely needed hard currency but also promoting an extravagant and ultimately disastrous series of building projects which have left Sarajevo bankrupt ever since.

The wealth of the 1970s – those western bankers who so foolishly invested in communism must I fear take some of the blame – has unfortunately resulted in whatever interior decoration the Austrians put into the Hotel Europa being ripped out and replaced by a glittering array of orange plastic light fittings and rust- and cherry-coloured carpets. But in the hotel's café, smoky and squalid, some link with the past was recalled as two Muslims, a violinist and a pianist, attempted, undeterred by their inadequate talents and a painfully out-of-tune piano, to render an arrangement of a well-known Lehar waltz from *The Merry Widow*. The crowd was oblivious to their efforts, produced with that tongue-between-the-teeth concentration which is the hallmark of the modest amateur. On closer inspection the pianist was found to be labouring under not only the disadvantages of his instrument but also the necessity of having to follow the score with one eye, the other being encased in a Gilbertian patch. With his high cheekbones and long nose he appeared the epitome of an off-duty Bosnian anarchist.

As I listened to the music I was addressed by a dark-eyed Bosnian girl with reams of thick curling black hair, a finely cut face and deep red generous lips, who assured me I was most fortunate to have hit upon a sunny day in Sarajevo. This Balkan beauty appeared to long for nothing more in life than sun. When there is no sun, she said, the smog is unbearable. I needed no convincing. The previous January in Sarajevo I had been asphyxiated by a heavy cloud of pollution, which only lifted to give way to sunshine several kilometres beyond the city. My dark-eyed companion was called Lydia and was about twenty-three. In defiance of prevailing modern custom in the city she saw no reason why she should not sit alone in the café of the Europa waiting for two friends to roll up later in the evening. These, when they arrived, both proved to be involved in a student magazine which was highly critical of communism and had helped to expose the antics of several communist businessmen-cum-politicians who had forged promissory notes and almost single-handedly emptied the province's coffers.

Of these the most celebrated was Fikret Abdič, the founder and manager of the Agrokomerc factory in northern Bosnia. Abdič had ruled his factory like a latter-day Lorenzo the Magnificent. He travelled between the building and his luxury Frank Lloyd Wright-style villa in a vehicle which was described as 'something out of the twenty-first century'. His arrest in 1987 had brought down scores of politicians and revealed all too vividly the ominously close twisted links between different families.

'The power and wealth of this republic is in no more than six or seven families,' Lydia explained before proceeding to paint a picture of a patriarchal society not unlike that which I imagined existed earlier this century in parts of Naples. Financial speculation was rife but whereas some in Bosnia might have expected such things to be in the hands of the Jewish inhabitants it was in Bosnia largely the occupation of Muslims. Half a mile from the Hotel Europa stood the 'Carringtonke' flats which had been named, on account of their opulence, after the American television series 'Dynasty'. These had cost 'millions' to build but were now left half empty because both builder and architect, to say nothing of part of the esteemed waiting list for such flats, were behind bars. 'No doubt if the Jews were running such deals the transactions would be more successful,' Lydia wryly commented.

All of these young Bosnians in the Hotel Europa possessed a quiet confidence which I had not so far encountered on my journey. There was none of the flashiness or bravado of the Montenegrins, just the unmistakable clarity of expression associated with the Serb. Not that Bosnian youth should be underestimated, for as everyone who has ever heard of Sarajevo knows, it was the youth of Bosnia which set the old Europe ablaze.

Not far from where the contemporary youth of the city talked to me a narrow street from the Hotel runs to the old Appel Quay, now called after several renamings Radičeviča Vojvode Stepe. Every visitor to Sarajevo, and I was no exception, gazes at some point at the spot where history was made. At the corner of the quay opposite what is now Princip Bridge spanning the sluggish Miljacka River there stands dressed in the bold angular lines of post-1918 national-ist architecture the Museum of the Young Bosnians, Mlada Bosna. On a pavement outside, two well-worn footsteps sunk an inch into a flagstone attempt to recall the precise position the twenty-year-old Gavrilo Princip took up before letting loose two rounds from his Browning pistol, killing the heir to the Austrian throne, Archduke Franz Ferdinand, and his wife the Duchess of Hohenberg on 28

76

June 1914. Inside the museum, empty and silent but for the crackle of pages of the museum attendant's magazine, there are a few mementoes of a different world. Some eyes will linger no doubt on the weatherbeaten faces of Princip's humble parents, peasants dressed in their Sunday best devoted to the order and stability of a world their son destroyed. In another corner there are 'relics of the Austrian oppression', but these amount to little more than a couple of telegrams and a photograph of manœuvres. More poignant is Princip's collar box, a crude if serviceable contraption, with a large stud of Serbian silver and lapis as its star attraction.

In Vienna I had of course seen the blood-stained uniform of the Archduke laid out in the black-curtained room which is still the high point of the Heeresgeschichtliches Museum. Now, surveying these relics, I recalled a hot summer's afternoon when in the company of friends I had cycled up to the old hunting lodge of the Archduke, the onion-domed schloss at Artstetten above the Danube a few miles from Melk. How different the world of the Erzherzog from the world of the man responsible for his downfall. At Artstetten the most disturbing relic of this difficult and, it is generally admitted, overbearing member of the Habsburg family is a banal vocabulary of Czech phrases presented to the Archduke as a young officer in Bohemia. The first sentence reads: *'Wie heisst du junge, Mädel?'* ('What is your name, little girl?') Every portrait and photograph of the Archduke in that grim castle and indeed elsewhere suggests that the reaction of any little girl to such a man uttering this phrase would be one of instinctive and overwhelming fear. Despite the awful and tragic consequences of the assassination it is difficult not to feel that somehow Princip was in his own naïve way the more agreeable protagonist of the drama.

That there was little love lost between the Archduke and the Emperor Franz Josef is well-known. Franz Ferdinand never found a way into the Emperor's closely guarded heart. After the collapse of the empire the story was put about that the Emperor had virtually connived at his heir's fate by sending him to what he knew was certain death in Bosnia. One source even quoted the Emperor as saying when he heard of the assassination: 'The Almighty cannot be defied with impunity. A divine will has re-established that order of things which I, alas, am not able to preserve.' This rather too pat utterance rings a little hollow though it has been quoted time and again by those willing to show that both by marrying beneath him and favouring a Trialist solution, bringing the Slavs into the dual Austro-Hungarian Empire, the Archduke was profoundly at odds with the Emperor's vision of his dynastic duties.

Certainly the risk of assassination must have been considered by the Emperor, who himself had miraculously escaped an attempt in Sarajevo only four years earlier. Bombs were always going off in Bosnia. Every year an attempt was made to kill the Governor, some high-ranking soldier or other representative of Habsburg rule. On 15 June 1910 an anarchist called Zerajič fired several bullets at the Governor of Bosnia on exactly the same spot as Princip fired his fateful shots. The first hit the step of the driver's seat, the second went through the roof of the coach near the Governor's eyes. The third would have hit him in the heart had he not in the meantime moved forward and had the driver not accelerated. The fourth hit the back of the coach at the height of the Governor's head, while the last bullet also hit the back of the coach. So all five bullets missed, but only just. Of such things is fate or, as some would have it, luck compounded.

Franz Ferdinand certainly knew the details of this attempt, as he also knew the circumstances of an earlier near-attempt on the Emperor's life. On 3 June 1910 Zerajič had got close enough to Franz Josef to shoot him dead but was struck by the venerable old age of his victim. 'When he saw the Emperor his hand could not draw his Browning from his pocket,' a contemporary relates. 'I could almost have touched him,' Zerajič was reported as saying at his trial. The Archduke's children later recalled their surprise on hearing that their father was to be sent to Sarajevo because 'it was known that only a miracle had saved the Emperor'. No miracles occurred to save the Archduke four years later, the entire day's proceedings moving inexorably to their conclusion almost as if indeed ordained by a higher order. To begin with, there were no soldiers to line the street as had happened when the Emperor had visited Sarajevo. In fact the Prefect of Police had barely 150 detectives to watch over the security of the royal entourage. When the imperial party of six cars came through the Appel Quay no fewer than six fanatical anarchists hoping to free Bosnia from Austrian rule awaited them. The first conspirator, Mehmed Hasič, failed to recognise the Archduke. Another was fooled by the presence of a gendarme who suddenly stood behind him. A third failed to shoot out of pity for the Duchess. A fourth, Popovič, said later, 'I don't know what happened but my courage just failed me.' Princip, however, had a first-class opportunity to shoot when the Archduke's car stopped for a moment, but he did not. In his excitement he too failed to recognise the Archduke. This temporary check however, serving as it did as a kind of dress rehearsal, may have proved decisive when the assassin found himself, half an hour later, presented with another opportunity.

It was left to the man whom all his fellow conspirators believed was unreliable to set the ball rolling. Nedeljko Cabrinovič asked a police agent, 'In which car is His Majesty?' The detective, ignoring his orders to watch the crowd rather than the cortège, replied, 'The third.' Cabrinovič took a bomb from his waist, knocked the detonator off against a lamppost, and threw the bomb at the green feathers of the Archduke's ceremonial hat. The bomb fell exactly behind him. 'At that very second,' Cabrinovič revealed at his trial, 'I saw the Archduke turning his cold and piercing glance on me.' Five seconds later the bomb exploded under the next car injuring a dozen of the crowd but only damaging the hand of one of the Archduke's aides.

Princip, who heard the explosion, saw the Archduke's car standing still but again failed to recognise him. As the police began clearing the quay, Princip crossed the street to Moritz Schiller's delicatessen where, he later said, 'I reflected where to wait in ambush because I knew from the newspapers where he should pass again.'

According to the official schedule the Archduke should have passed from the Appel quay through the narrow Franz Josef Street, but at the town hall he changed his route so that he could return straight along the quay to the military hospital to visit one of his wounded staff. Had this new route been followed it is likely the grim sequence of events which now took place could have been avoided. But in a singularly Austrian piece of organisational *schlamperei* no one in the Archduke's entourage or among the police thought of informing the driver.

Only the owner of the Archduke's car, Count Harrach, who had travelled behind the driver, changed his position so as to shield the Archduke and stood on the left running-board eyeing the crowd along the embankment. But this worthy move only proved to seal the Archduke's fate, for when the car reached Franz Josef Street the first vehicles followed the original plan and turned up the narrow road. As the Archduke's car followed and then attempted to reverse back to the quay, Princip found himself staring at his prey from a distance of less than fifteen yards. Had Count Harrach not been thinking of a possible attack from the embankment and been standing on the other running-board, it is quite likely that the shots would have missed their mark – albeit at the expense of that gentle nobleman's life. As it was, Princip found he had an unobstructed field of vision.

A detective, seeing the arm level to shoot, rushed to interrupt it but was kneed in the groin by Mihailjo Pušava, a young Bosnian supporter and a tall handsome man who sang at the opera. Franz Ferdinand's fate had been sealed. After Princip had fired straight at the Duchess, his second shot caught the Archduke just under the star of rank on his collar.

Count Harrach takes up the story: 'As the car reversed rapidly, a thin stream of blood sprayed from His Highness's mouth on to my right cheek. As I was pulling out my handkerchief to wipe the blood away from his mouth, the Duchess cried out to him, "In heaven's name what has happened to you?" And with that she slid off the seat and lay on the floor of the car, with her face between his knees. I had no idea she had been hit and presumed she had fainted with fright. Then I heard His Imperial Highness say "Sophie, Sophie, don't die. Live for the children!" At that I seized the Archduke by the collar of his uniform to stop his head dropping forward and asked him if he was in great pain. He answered me quite distractedly, "It's nothing!" His face began to twist somewhat but he went on repeating six or seven times ever more faintly as he lost consciousness, "It's nothing", then after a short pass there was a violent choking sound caused by the bleeding. It stopped as we reached the Konak.'*

Twenty minutes later both of Princip's victims were dead. Asked by elements of the crowd which set about him with their fists who he was, Princip is said to have replied quietly, 'I am a Serbian hero.'

---

* Statement by Count Harrach to the Court of Inquiry on the day of the assassination.

In the Mlada Bosna museum, the photographs of Princip portray a scrawny, almost pathetic youth, the last man one would have expected to be the instrument which ultimately humbled an empire. That he was able to do so was due more to sheer luck than anything else, for the narrative of the Sarajevo assassination shows that it was one of the most amateur regicides of all time. Musing in the sunlight over Princip's collar stud I recalled Blanka's oft-repeated words, last used to dispatch an English girl from my mind. 'What could such a person know of the fear of God?' At the time, though I had been brought up as a Catholic I was not sure myself what the phrase really meant. But no one pondering in Sarajevo the sequence of events on that fateful day can fail to believe that we are indeed 'like flies to the gods'.

7 THE VIRGIN ON THE KARST

'How *do* you get to Madgers?' the tall, handsome girl of impeccable
White Russian descent asked me with suitably Farm Street aloofness. We had just found Sarajevo's Ali Pasha mosque, built in 1561
for the Governor of Bosnia, Hadim Ali Pasha. The mosque is
curious because it is designed in a classical style which was carefully
restored by the Austrians in 1874. To be questioned on a Catholic
shrine in the heart of Islam is like talking of sin in a presbytery. It
has been a few years now since the Knights of Malta exchanged
their *Almanachs de Gotha* for Cook's far more readable European
railway timetables and sought out a village in Herzegovina called
Medjugorije. It is a strange departure for those who, cloaked and
decorated in their sovereign order, are accustomed only to the most
organised and unspontaneous of pilgrimages to the great city of
Lourdes. Communism is, rightly, anathema to them all, but yet
they have been found to step into the land of the anti-Christ to see
what remains today of one of the most controversial and extraordinary of all Catholic phenomena in Europe.

In 1981 in the small village of Medjugorije, some children had a
vision. They believed, as the sun was setting on that harsh Karst
landscape above Mostar, sparsely populated save for a few families
and some Franciscans, that the Virgin Mary was standing before
them. Not only did the apparition move but she also spoke, bidding
them to return each evening to hear her messages. These, speaking
of love and charity and calling for more prayers for peace on earth,
were taken down from the children each evening and posted up on
the church door. And so, uninterrupted by the passage of time and
the invasion of the village by tens of thousands of pilgrims each
year, this extraordinary scene has continued each evening to this
day, even though the children who originally received the messages
have grown up and many have left the village. Mass hysteria, the
sceptics argue; Franciscan foolery, says the Bishop of Mostar; 'We
saw visions,' counters the devout English Catholic lady. In Vienna,

a friend had given me the name of a cousin, an Archduchess who had virtually decamped a few years ago at the age of twenty-five to Herzegovina to be as close as possible to the visions. Others had also given up friends, jobs and material pleasure to be near to the village which once boasted only a few houses, but is now developing more rapidly than any boom town in North America before the war.

Careful examination of a very detailed map shows that Medjugorije lies just south of Mostar. Even in 1988, when the place was already the most frequently visited spot in Jugoslavia, no official map revealed its location. In Sarajevo's cathedral I asked a young closely cropped priest how to get there and was instructed tersely: 'Take the afternoon express to Mostar. This should get in at about 6. At 6.20 there is a bus. It does not go to Medjugorije but if you take it ask for the village and they will drop you a few miles away. Then you must walk.'

It was June, scorching heat, and Herzegovina, unlike rolling Bosnia, is the hottest place on the peninsula in high summer. But the timing of the bus sounded suitable, for the sun would be past its worst and yet still high enough to help guide the way for the last few miles. One lightly packed grip would be enough and should suffice for a few days.

From Sarajevo to Mostar the distance is eighty-four and a half miles, but whereas Sarajevo is up in the hills Mostar is low on the coast and the railway line must traverse a mountain district of quite breathtaking drama. 'You will see,' nodded an old ticket collector at the station, in broken German, 'the Austrian engineer who built this line was a genius. He just let his donkey loose and followed it up the mountain, laying the path of the track behind it. Only in this way would it have been possible to build such a line.'

For once there was no Slav hyperbole and for once the station appeared divested of its habitual soldiery. The express, one of the prestige trains of the Jugoslav railways, was attended by white-gloved stewardesses who not only showed me to a seat but also provided coffee, orange juice and a bunch of grapes at regular intervals throughout the journey. Television sets blared away in one of the carriages though these were completely upstaged by the grandeur of the scenery which opened up barely ten minutes out of Sarajevo. After threading, as Baedeker would say, a pretty wooded

1. Countess Blanka von Korvin-Giustiniani

2. Sir Nevile Henderson

3. The Montenegrin Royal Family, 1910

4. Baron Josef Jellačič von Buzim

5. The Jellačič Statue, Zagreb

6. Baron Gottfried von Banfield, the 'Eagle of Trieste'

7. Ksenja Treščec von Branski

8. Sarajevo

9. Dubrovnik

10. Angel from the Račič Chapel

11. The Račič Chapel

12. Dessa Trevisan,
veteran *Times* lady in the
Balkans

13. Pilgrims at the church at Medjugorije

14. J. D. Bourchier

valley, the line quickly descends towards Tarčin. Here the peaks of the great Ivan Planina rise up and the line promptly begins to ascend. Originally toothed rails had to be used to accomplish this journey but today the long electric locomotive painted yellow and maroon and modelled on a French engine of the 1970s takes all this in its stride. The gradient is at its steepest, Baedeker tells us, between Rastelica and Ivan (2,870 feet). The ridge of the Ivan Planina is not only the frontier between Bosnia and Herzegovina, it is also the watershed between the Black Sea and the Adriatic. It is pierced by a 700-yard tunnel and the train enters this long cool cavern before emerging in bright sunlight in as wild and romantic a country as is possible in the Balkans.

Colonel Barry noted of the people of Herzegovina: 'The hard surroundings of the land here, altogether more desolate than the regions of the same character in Dalmatia, bring out all the manhood in the land. The Herzegovinian cuts a splendid figure, intelligent, industrious and forceful, in striking contrast with the indolent loutish air too common among the peasantry of Bosnia. He would rather die at 40 in his windswept hut among the rocks, the home of his kindred, than take the bribe of gold to die enriched in some palace of the Far West.' Of such heroic manhood there is little sign. Indeed there is little sign of anything for the train now rattles down the valley of the Treščanica gathering so much speed that the other comparable descent of a railway to the Adriatic, that into Trieste, seems stately by comparison. At any moment as it hurtles towards each tunnel (at the other end of which it emerges facing the opposite direction), the train appears all too capable of parting company with its rails. At Konjica the first of several old Turkish buildings can be seen straddling the Narenta River, which the train now follows still at breakneck speed.

Whatever the temperature in Sarajevo, the thermometer will register ten degrees higher here. The Narenta valley has never since 1878 failed to excite travellers. Bordered on all sides by dramatic peaks, the line now reaches Jablanica, a well-situated jumping-off point for climbers, though I suspect in cooler seasons. Beyond an even more picturesque defile the line crosses the Glogošnica valley with a splendid panoramic view of the mountains. But this glimpse of distant peaks is brief. At the end of another tunnel the Great Defile or Gorge of Narenta, with waterfalls and distant views of other wild gorges to right and left, awaits us. By the time we reach Mostar, a few miles further on, the most ardent enthusiast of mountain railways will have had his appetite satisfied. If the train continues it will reach a station some miles north of Dubrovnik. From there a fine coast road whose principal delight apart from the azure sea is a remarkable plane tree of colossal proportions, reputedly planted in medieval times, leads in a couple of hours to the pearl of the Adriatic.

Fifty years ago, Mostar could quite plausibly be described as the 'Land's End of orientalism' swept on three sides by the Atlantic of western civilisation. Today the walls have been breached and there is precious little of the Orient left. The Roman Catholic cathedral outshines the thirty-odd mosques which, with the exception of the Kavadjoz Bey, are of little merit. Mohammedism, perfectly able to resist the missionary, has been weakened by the Party, blue jeans and the car. The religion of conquest, of female seclusion, of the lascivious harem has become submerged here into the atheist creed of commerce and progress.

There is now little to be seen of the city apart from the great bridge and, on the other side of it, the old stone prison from which less than a hundred years ago many a prisoner of the Turks, Albanians, Serbs or Bosnians fought to escape – usually quite successfully, if contemporary sources are accurate. The bridge dates from the fifteenth century but was rebuilt and remodelled on the orders of Suleiman the Magnificent in 1566 shortly before he set forth on his famous expedition to besiege Vienna. The architect was Mimar Heyrudin, whom it is pointed out was a disciple of Mimar Sirian, author of the great minarets of Constantinople.

Not far from the prison end of the bridge a *kavana* under some vines offered for the first time since entering Bosnia-Herzegovina some refreshing *drinkable* white wine. The vines here are of the low, stumpy variety and the best wine is of two kinds, a white wine called Zilabka or Gubic not unlike dry white Bordeaux and a ruby red not unlike Montepulciano, 'somewhat rough but justly celebrated' as Baedeker dubbed it. Both Herzegovinian wines are, however, high in alcohol content. That wines can be grown at all in a climate of almost lethal extremes is remarkable. For however hot the barren area of the province is, there is in winter and sometimes even in summer the threat of the Bora, that harsh wind first encountered in Trieste, which in winter sends the mercury scuttling below the zero mark. Here in Mostar the Bora is even noisier, howling and blowing in its full majesty through the Mostar valley, which is shaped like a trumpet almost one feels in order to maximise its effect. Mostar's valley is indeed the Bora's megaphone, and above the town the small villages appear crouched even in summer to avoid the wind's onslaught.

At the bus station, mention of the name Medjugorije provoked a variety of reactions ranging from indulgent sympathy to unequivocal pity tinged with contempt. The latter was more prevalent when on the bus I asked for a one-way ticket to the shrine. Whichever way the tens of thousands of pilgrims come to 'Madgers' it was certainly not by this bus, which slowly wound its way up the mountainside depositing a variety of Herzegovinian farmers who, however god-fearing, clearly saw little point in visiting the self-appointed holiest place in Jugoslavia. The happy smiling curiosity of Assisi or Mariazell was grimly absent among the passengers who seemed resolutely indifferent to my pilgrimage.

Dozing in the late afternoon heat, I was suddenly aware of a hand pressing my arm. I opened my eyes to see a leathery-faced old woman jabbering away at me imploring my immediate departure from the bus which had ground to a halt at a small fork in the road around which there was very little, if any, habitation. 'Is this the place?' 'Yes, yes, little walk now,' returned the woman, and in a cloud of dust the bus drove off leaving me, I reflected not for the first time, alone in a place bereft of any indication as to where my next steps lay.

To the south, the sky was Adriatic blue – was the sea just over that furthest hill? To the west the setting sun was a burnished fire-ball still giving off a devastating heat. But apart from this there was not only no one to be seen, there was no breeze, hardly any vegetation, no houses, certainly no shelter and, most disconcerting of all, no signposts. The absence of any fellow-pilgrims was also disturbing. Had I mispronounced my destination so effectively as to place myself more than the 'few' miles away from the village? At this point, almost as if in answer to the question, there came echoing over the hills the sound of bells, so my dilemma was solved by those distant Balkan campanologists.

The road had tarmac though of veteran quality. At times it

petered out into a dust track. At other times it assumed pretensions towards a highway of no mean dimensions. But dust track or road, of traffic there was no sign. Only Karst. Bleak inescapable Karst. After about half an hour there was no doubt that the bells sounded louder but at the same time no hint was available that anyone lived at or around this still invisible church.

After the third or fourth bend, the landscape suddenly dropped slightly towards the distant ridges of peaks and there in the middle foreground, sheltered on one side by a hill, rose two campanili. In the bright sunlight it was a welcoming sight, though not, I remember noting even then, a particularly warm one. The bright white stone of the church bore no relation to the brown and grey landscape. From a distance it seemed clearly of late nineteenth-century or perhaps even later construction. It was crude, sharp and angular, and as twilight set in and the sky became French grey in colour it resembled nothing so much as a giant pair of sharp teeth. Still the bells rang their merry rounds. There is something incomparably rustic about walking along a country lane with only a few possessions to a distant building which one can hear more clearly than one can see.

There was, too, something exhilarating in eventually reaching the church to find several hundred people standing outside deep in prayer during a sung mass. Most of them were young and many were Italian girls who had travelled by bus and boat from southern Italy. At the rear of the church stood a group of pale, straw-haired Bavarians, faces rapt. Outside, more young girls between the ages of fourteen and seventeen queued in a line to kneel at the feet of a number of buck-teethed Franciscan monks. One pretty and devout girl after another, faces charged with emotion, knelt with their heads towards the brown cloth as friars heard confession. Having always been careful to avoid where possible manifestations of hysteria, on reflection I found this sight rather disturbing. There was without doubt a powerful whiff of the holy, and as I found later walking across the barren limestone and up the treacherously unsheltered hills, there are few places in the Balkans so conducive to solitude and prayer. But the sheer concentration of unquestioning adulation and worship round the church would, I think, be found suffocating by the most spiritual of observers. And everything which happened later bore this out.

That evening, an Austrian aristocrat who had given up everything to come and live in the house where I was lodged embarked on a eulogy of the place so extreme and emotional that I, after the first half hour, began to entertain serious doubts as to her sanity. But then how difficult it must be for those who turn their backs on the material to retain a sense of perspective and balance when discussing the sublime with a stranger. No one could doubt their sincerity. And no one who has seen the Medjugorije children's eyes follow as one the – to us invisible – passage of the Virgin Mary across the small room in which she has chosen to appear, can also doubt that *something* is taking place. But however genuine the vision, the side effects of such phenomena do not necessarily show up humanity at its best.

This was underlined by a curious incident which increased my sense of unease. A young Englishman appeared after the service at about 7.30 p.m. asking to see one of the senior monks, a man of about forty, who was moving among the adoring crowds with the air of a minor deity himself. In his late twenties the Englishman was modest and indeed, compared to most of the people encountered, remarkably sane; he had travelled more than twenty-four hours just to talk to the monk, whom he hoped would offer guidance on a number of issues. Could he meet the Father at 8.30 p.m.? No, that would be impossible the monk replied, patting the head of a young Italian girl who fawned on him with dark eyes. 'I am going tonight to Mostar.' 'What about now?' asked the pilgrim. 'Too busy I'm afraid until 8 o'clock.' 'And then?' asked the youth, desperately hoping for the 8 to 8.30 slot. 'Then? Why then I am going to Mostar,' returned the monk. 'Father is going to Mostar,' chorused the girls protectively.

It was about 9.30 p.m. by the time I reached my quarters for the next two days, a vine-clad villa run by an engaging man who also drove a bus, did some farming and appeared quite detached from the entire Medjugorije phenomenon. He himself rarely attended the services, he confided, though everyone else in the house did, including yet another scion of an ancient Central European family. During this talk with him in the kitchen, I was much amused to hear a knock on the door and see emerging from the dark garden the unmistakable figure of the same monk who had proved so elusive to the English pilgrim earlier that evening and who was supposed at this very moment to be at least half-way to Mostar. Recognising me as someone who had witnessed his earlier excuses I'm glad to say he was humble enough to show signs of embarrassment as he disappeared upstairs to spend what the *padrone* called 'two hours of spiritual instruction' with a pious lady who had exchanged the spurious glamour of Vienna for the attentions of the worldly Franciscans. Nothing that I saw in Medjugorije during the following week ever quite dispelled the suspicion that the Franciscans, faced with minds that were naïve and pliable, were not beyond the well-tried monastic arts of manipulation.

My host refused to be drawn on the subject, preferring to dwell on the rapidly changing infrastructure of the village. The communist government, aware that vast hard currency revenues were being lost by virtue of the fact that the state was in no way involved in Medjugorije, was determined to cash in sooner or later. 'We will be taxed out of existence,' he said, 'taxed for a farm, taxed for a paying guest and taxed just because we live within a ten-mile radius of the church.' The communists were also reputed to be keen to build up what they euphemistically called the village 'resource'. When I was there Medjugorije still had that magnificent unspoilt air of being little more than a church, a presbytery and, a good ten-minute walk along a road, a vine-clad café. But later that year shops and stalls were to open in front of the church and there were plans afoot to build a hotel half way up the Calvary Hill, a favourite if punishing pilgrim route near the church. The blissful evening peace after the bus-loads of pilgrims had departed threatened to be shattered first by ambitious construction work and then by the inevitable panoply of that which every communist regards as essential to his happiness: a (no doubt described as modest) night-life. Medjugorije's future in one sense remains far from bright.

The Vatican is believed to be largely in favour of what is happening in Medjugorije, though it has treated the events there with the customary caution it reserves for such 'psychic phenomena'. Thanks to the remarkable personality of Pope John Paul II, the tortuous and often difficult relations between communism and Catholicism have never been more prominent on the agenda of international affairs. If communism is in its death-throes, can Catholicism rise to the challenge and fill the vacuum left by the departure of a crude, meaningless ideology whose very obsolescence and irrelevance to man's problems has made it so valueless in the closing years of the twentieth century? Catholicism has the power to mobilise the masses, as the huge numbers of visitors to Medjugorije show, and I cannot help thinking that the fact that those visions of the Medjugorije children appeared for the first time shortly after Marshal Tito's death is somehow significant. If the Virgin Mary is appearing in a communist country perhaps the cypher of her messages means something more pagan: look about you, a godless system responsible for cruelty and the misery of countless people in the Balkans is about to disintegrate. Unless you replace it with one based on moral strength and draw the appropriate lessons, you will only experience more misery.

To reconcile such speculations with what I had seen of the protagonists in Medjugorije took longer than the two-day journey back through Bosnia.But I recalled these thoughts when later I found myself gazing at spent cartridges in Jugoslavia's most troubled province: Kossovo.

8 PRUSSIANS OF THE BALKANS

Somewhere beneath the window, the din began again. The syn-copated beat of a bass drum, the blaring out-of-tune trumpet and a shrill clarinet, all competing over an erratic and congested euphonium, played only one tune:

The harmonies and embellishments of the trumpeter and euphonium players would I think have defeated the attempts of the most conscientious musician to record them. It was clear that none of the players – swarthy, ragged men – had ever read a note of music and were offering a host of variations on a theme which had been passed down to them by an aural rather than written tradition.

The insistent rhythm cut through the hot air of a balmy spring evening in Belgrade. Along Terasia, still the most attractive boul-evard in the city, despite the efforts of the German, British and American air forces at various stages of the war to destroy it, the gypsies played to a growing audience, though not all were sympathetic. A colleague weary after long hours of travel and eager to sleep opened the window two bays along on the sixth floor of the Hotel Moskva and emptied the contents of a bottle of mineral water over the musicians who, when it reached them in a small deluge, only invested their tune with fruitier harmonies for a couple of bars. The band was clearly used to the possibility of an unsym-

93

pathetic response from high buildings and simply wheeled a few yards to the right to place themselves out of range. The clarinettist, however, began to steal glances at regular intervals in a heavenward direction; for a split second the black and angry eyes met mine before catching the smiling face of my neighbour nearby.

I had first heard this band six months earlier on a foggy autumn afternoon near the Konak, as the former Governor's residence is called, overlooking the Danube, where many a leafy Serbian promenade resounds to buskers. They are invariably gypsies, the Serbs' capacity for instrumental music being somewhat restricted; so limited in fact that the Serbs' usual response to these buskers' music is to ignore the musicians or to peer somewhat foolishly at their instruments.

The reaction to this band, however, was different. A small crowd gathered, money was searched for in a number of moth-eaten pockets, from which coins and even notes were duly produced for the benefit of the performers. Far from decrying the monotonous cacophony of this memorable if repetitive tune, the audience appeared to crave for more. A few days later in a restaurant a most sophisticated musician began to play the same tune. A week afterwards almost every café along Terasia, with the honourable exception of the octogenarian orchestra playing excruciating Strauss waltzes in the Hotel Moskva, resounded to the same melody.

As its rhythm suggests this was an old Serbian war song and the words, which I heard only once in a tavern cellar, called for Serbians to avenge their defeat by the Turks at the Battle of Kossovo Field. It was on this 'Field of the Black Birds' that on 28 June 1389 the fate of the Balkan peninsula was decided for centuries when a Turkish army annihilated the Serbs.

No word was – and is – more frequently on Serbian lips than Kossovo. The then autonomous province between Serbia, Albania and Montenegro largely inhabited by ethnic Albanians was daily a cause for humiliation, anger and frustration. The facts for every Belgrade Serb were simple: the majority of the province's population might well be ethnic Albanians but they had no right to lord it over 200,000 Serbs who were being virtually forced to abandon their villages – villages which had for centuries been Serbian and which were the cradle of Serbian culture. The response to this crisis had been, as so often in the Balkans, one of hysteria. There were no excuses, no extenuating circumstances for the Albanians. Day after day, week after week, the Serbian press, once the most liberal and open-minded in Jugoslavia, drove the message home: the ethnic Albanians were not only anti-socialist, counter-revolutionary and anti-Jugoslav; they were semi-literate barbarians, oriental, untrustworthy bandits whose habits and morals beggared description in modern Jugoslavia. A time of reckoning was coming. The gypsy musicians, with their infallible intuition as to which way the wind was blowing, were playing what most Serbs wanted to hear. Older Serbs knew what the martial melody meant and no northern European could imagine that the solution to the 'Kossovo problem' could under these circumstances be anything but violent.

That very evening, the band outside the Hotel Moskva was already playing to a captive audience of several tens of thousands of Serbs who had gathered for a mass demonstration in sympathy with the beleaguered Kossovo Serbs. From every corner of the republic they had poured in, disrupting traffic but marching in an orderly way outside the Parliament to hold their '*Miting*'. It was the climax of scores of similar if more modest meetings held throughout Serbia. At each one of these the slogans were ominously similar: 'Hang Vlassi', a reference to the detested Albanian leader in Kossovo, Azem Vlassi; 'Long live Slobo', an allusion to the popular Serbian leader Slobodan Milosevič, whose first name also means freedom in Serbian. Entire villages and towns and now the city of Belgrade had been brought to a standstill. There was, however, to observers who had been to more than one of these demonstrations, something disturbingly familiar about the routine, language and, most sinister of all, the faces of many of the protagonists involved. A travelling circus of organisers and rabble-rousers was clearly available to tap frustration and discontent not only over Kossovo but also over the economic crisis of Jugoslavia itself.

This economic crisis had by the summer of 1989 caused inflation to run at more than 900 per cent and, more disturbingly, had created the highest unemployment in Europe. As every 'meeting' showed all too vividly, there were thousands of people in each Jugoslav city, town and village who had nothing better to do than to turn up and be lectured to by others who, whatever their motives, were highly subversive.

In Kraljevo, the old Serbian fortress town south of Belgrade where I had first witnessed a 'meeting', the presence of so many teenagers in the crowd was profoundly depressing. Here, as if in an echo of pre-war fanaticism, the crudest and basest instincts of man were being inflamed and exploited for political ends. Despite a downpour which must have soaked everyone to the skin, a crowd of more than 20,000 gathered, stood ankle-deep in mud and listened with rapt attention. Something about the combination of smiling rustic faces and awful weather recalled a Dorset point-to-point, but there was nothing so harmless in the language or sentiments expressed here.

Was Kossovo the reason for all this? I asked a young bearded man I found myself standing next to. He turned round with that gentle expression so often encountered among the Balkan Slavs but which frequently appears curiously out of context in an atmosphere tinged with violence. 'Reasons? Not Kossovo,' he murmured slowly with great deliberation. 'Not Kossovo. Many reasons. Many reasons.'

In Belgrade the crowd beneath my window was less vague. Here, too, it began to rain but undeterred even by the retreat of the musicians a crowd of about five hundred gathered in the middle of the road with banners and giant posters, not of the late Marshal Tito, whose image is ubiquitous in this country, but of Slobodan Milosevič, portraits of whose chubby face were rapidly beginning to outnumber those of the more familiar and bemedalled Marshal. There were also large numbers of red flags, as if to confirm that dissatisfaction in Jugoslavia was not *anti*-communist but aimed at what are considered to be abuses of communism. 'That's never communism,' a driver had pointed out to me as we raced past the luxury villas of the Bosnian party bosses at Neum, along the Adriatic coast, pouring scorn on those who ruled Jugoslavia today.

Most of the rabble-rousers beneath the Moskva were young and expensively dressed in leather jackets – a whiff of foreign funding here perhaps? At one stage a senior police officer attempted to persuade the crowd to break up and move off but his efforts were met by boos and jeers. Eventually one of the mob leaders jumped up between the policeman and another mobster and began to employ the most dramatic gesticulations. It was almost as if he were performing a mime for the mentally retarded. For five minutes, one extravagant gesture followed another: hands together pleading one moment; hands outstretched, palms upward, the next. At each juncture the object of these attentions, the other mob leader, answered back with even more compelling and baroque gestures. After another ten minutes, the crowd moved sullenly off. They had been told by their hero, Milosevič, that their time was ripe. No one had the right to beat them. He, Slobo, would look after their interests as he had looked after them in the past. He would ensure that the unfairness and inequality from which the Serbs suffered would be rectified and that the forces of law and order – which he controlled – would not raise a finger to stop them.

Later that evening in the venerable palais which houses the Serbian Writers' Club I listened, as I had done so many times before, to the judgement of *The Times*' veteran correspondent in Belgrade, the formidable Madam Trevisan. Dessa Trevisan, who knows more about the intricacies of Balkan politics than anyone else alive, summed up Milosevič in a series of dazzling verbal thrusts which left him, like a fencing master's dummy, cut to ribbons after a few minutes' practice with a sharpened foil. Long before any other correspondent in Belgrade, Dessa had 'spotted' Milosevič and seen him for the threat to potential Jugoslav democracy he is and as the man who would determine the country's future. Long before anyone had even heard of the man and I suspect a considerable time before his name appeared in a Foreign Office telegram, Dessa had not only sized him up but made it her business to have regular luncheons with him. Only someone supremely and uniquely well informed on the detail of Jugoslavia's tangled maze of politics could have pulled this off.

Even in the later months of 1988, when a series of crises brought scores of so-called 'well-informed' correspondents to Belgrade from every country in northern Europe and beyond, Dessa still proved the value – so often underrated today in British newspaper offices – of a local correspondent deeply familiar with the history and affairs of the country involved. One evening after something like three hundred correspondents had spent more than twelve hours in various states of chain-smoking and inescapable *ennui* awaiting the result of a crucial Central Committee meeting it was Dessa who alone knew the significance of the Committee's deliberations. The journalists patiently awaited the lugubrious statements of the Committee spokesman but when he announced, with a gesture designed

to impart extreme gravitas to the occasion, that a man named
Skrebič (of whose existence no one was aware) had been ousted,
there was only a nonplussed silence. After what seemed like five
uneasy minutes, Dessa's cut-glass voice rang out: 'Of course! I told
you so. Skrebič!' For the ensuing half hour she was besieged by
reporters: she was their sole source of enlightenment.

Madam Trevisan's lunches with Mr Milosevič had continued
despite her increasingly hostile line to his activities and his
unprincipled gagging – described by one diplomat in typically
anodyne Foreign Office jargon as shameful – of the Serbian press.
Her latest encounter with Milosevič however had proved a particularly bruising experience for him and she doubted very much
whether there would be any further dates. On sitting down next to
her, the politician had eyed her coldly and, quoting from a recent
Times article, said, 'Miss Trevisan, according to a friend of mine in
London, you have compared me to Mussolini'. There ensued a
pause described to me by a witness as 'electric'. 'That's entirely
incorrect, Mr Milosevič,' answered Dessa, hissing like a dragon. 'I
admire Mussolini enormously. I did not compare you to Mussolini,
I merely compared your *posture* to Mussolini; I actually compared
you to the Ayatollah!'

From this crippling blow the man who is the epitome of strength
and power to millions of Serbs may never have fully recovered,
though by the time the pudding was served he was almost, according
to another observer, his old grimly confident self.

Others who had encountered this man agreed with Dessa that he
remained something of an enigma. His wife, however, was more
easily read. An orthodox communist who loathes champagne and
caviar, she was quoted as saying that the days of capitalism were
numbered, a remarkable comment for someone to make in 1989
when the whole of Eastern Europe was waking up to the fact that
the tenets of Marx were in the doldrums. In the Balkans, the
influence of the politician's wife is inordinate, as the recent state of
Romania painfully revealed. Until the west learned the truth about
Elene Ceausescu they may have been unaware that in the east
of Europe, from Poland in the north to Bulgaria well south of
Mitteleuropa, the female of the species is quite often deadlier than
the male.

Whatever views were held by those around the candlelit table in the Writers' Club, elsewhere in Belgrade Mr Milosevič was regarded with unquestioning obedience. The Serbs are not I think naturally docile or even naïve people. Milosevič's popularity had to be earned, however well organised his rabble rousers. That he was capable of doing this reveals that whatever his weaknesses he at least possesses two qualities essential in Serbian politics. The first of these is without doubt ruthlessness. For the first time since the terrible days of the late Marshal Tito's Stalinist police chief Rankovič, those who oppose the top politician are liable not only to removal from the corridors of power but also to arrest and imprisonment. Secondly, it is quite clear that Milosevič also has some flair for public speaking, though to describe it as oratory is perhaps to put it too high. A driver who took me to the small Serbian village of Saraorci gave me a two-hour lecture on Milosevič's merits which when stripped of Balkan hyperbole boiled down simply to the statement: 'He is a very *clear* man'; 'clear' meaning in this sense unambiguous, unequivocal. This quality, intangible to western visitors, is of overwhelming importance to the Serbs.

There are other factors too behind the man's success; factors which throughout the twentieth century have lain behind the power of demagogues. It was apparent in Belgrade in 1989 that whatever the affluence of the bourgeois communists who filled the Writers' Club – needless to say few if any of whom had ever wielded a pen other than to sign a cheque – poverty and despair were on the increase in the country. Decades of corruption and inertia, even when mitigated by the charisma and political gifts of a man like Tito, must eventually lead to chaos and bitterness. Sir Nevile Henderson had often quoted King Alexander's remark: 'My country needs forty years of peace to establish an honest bureaucracy.' This, Jugoslavia had enjoyed – but under communists. In Belgrade and elsewhere in Jugoslavia the effects of hyper-inflation had been the same as the effects of hyper-inflation everywhere. A few speculators – mostly those with access to foreign currency – were growing extremely prosperous while the rest of the population was losing its hard-earned savings by the minute. For the boot-blacks, taxi drivers and factory workers, life was becoming, increasingly, an exhausting struggle.

Between the Writers' Club next to the Opera House and the Hotel Moskva, the National Museum rises in a large square which is always, even without the benefit of Mr Milosevič and Serbian agitation, filled with a large crowd. It is a handsome francophile turn-of-the-century building built with that Beaux Arts swagger which underlines the strong ties with Paris enjoyed by the Balkans before the First World War. Inside is an impressive collection of early twentieth-century Serbian art which combines the colour of the Impressionists with the picturesque subject matter of the Balkans. Here is an escape into a more civilised Serbia where among the portraits of Marko Murat, a softer land, more primitive than today's Serbia but more fired by idealism and culture, is portrayed.

In the narrow streets below the museum towards Skadaria, the old quarter of small cobbled steps, I took a narrow road lined with peeling stucco houses of two or three storeys. In one of them I knew there lived a fine Serbian lady whose father had commanded the garrison in Belgrade when the Austrians invaded in 1914. Several years before I had visited her in these rooms divided by curtains and filled with Art Nouveau furniture and silk-covered sofas, to be given Turkish coffee and rakir before setting off for Herzegovina. My hostess then as now embodied all the positive traits of the Serbian character – tremendous dignity, warmth and a powerful spiritual strength and integrity – but even she could not see the Albanian point of view and the fact that hysteria now had the Serbs in its withering grip. Nevertheless, with the framed photographs of old Serbian officers gazing down on me I was treated to the most rational and tolerant defence of the Serbs' position in Kossovo to date.

The problem, as she saw it, had begun in 1941 with the Axis invasion of Jugoslavia. The frontier between Kossovo and Albania had been opened as the Italians poured into their new protectorate. This had boosted the numbers of Albanians living in Kossovo, and after the war they not surprisingly chose to remain rather than return to the red terror of Enver Hoxha's partisans in Tirana. From the end of the war they had, thanks to the highest birthrate in Europe, slowly gained in number until they believed they should enjoy self-determination. In 1989 a population of 1.75 million people could not be wished away or expelled. Somehow a compromise had to be found.

Standing up like a 1930s building in a Superman comic, the

Belgrade Officers' Club in the heart of the capital behind the Parliament is an unlikely place for making such a compromise. But not for nothing were the Serbs dubbed by Churchill the Prussians of the Balkans, and like Prussia in the eighteenth century, Serbia today respects the army. Indicative of the army's feeling that it is a law unto itself was a brand new and lavish Black Aston Martin parked, with extravagant contempt for local parking regulations, almost across the steps leading up to the fine portico. 'It's about time someone clipped these people's wings,' a resident correspondent remarked at this sight, but I was not so sure. Just as in the old Austrian Empire it was the army which ultimately guaranteed the multi-national state, so too in Jugoslavia the army is the only authority which speaks in the name of Jugoslavia as a federation. The federal government is lamentably weak. It remains to be seen how many generals will follow Milosevič's path to Armageddon and how many will sacrifice Serbian nationalism to remain faithful to their oaths and a broader ideal. No doubt they are divided and it would not be surprising to find lurking in the rooms of this club some retired officer of sufficient intelligence to be capable of anticipating the country's break-up, like the ill-fated Colonel Apis and his shadowy movement known as the Black Hand, implicated in the assassination of Archduke Franz Ferdinand in Sarajevo in 1914.

From the Officers' Club it is only a brisk walk along the Knez Mihailova pedestrian avenue with its discreet bookshops to the most dramatic and certainly most pleasant part of the city, the old fortifications and the great meeting-point of the Danube and the Sava which flow beneath what was for centuries Turkey's westernmost frontier. Here Prince Eugène, Marlborough's ally at Blenheim, had led his troops, drums and bands, accompanying their remorseless march up to the fortress. His 'Austrian army awfully arrayed boldly by battery besieged Belgrade' and in 1717 he captured the city from the Turks so that with the Treaty of Passarowitz soon after, large areas of present-day Serbia and Romania including Belgrade became Austrian. Although parts of the surrounding territory remained Austrian, Belgrade a few years later reverted to Turkish rule. The solid masonry of the fortress, which has withstood the First and Second World Wars, is a familiar sight throughout the Habsburg lands and the double-headed eagle is visible on similar red brick arches as far east as Alba Julia in Romania and as far north as Cracow in Poland.

The Military Museum which is housed here is an amusing collection of bits and pieces. Outside there is a splendid Austrian Skoda 30.5cm mortar similar to that which demolished the Belgian forces in 1914 and played such havoc with the Russians in 1915. Nearby stands the most successful artillery piece of the Second World War, also a piece of German technology, the formidable German anti-aircraft 88mm gun which thanks to its flexible trajectory could also act as an anti-tank gun.

Inside the museum, there are detailed plans of what was perhaps Belgrade's finest hour; its resistance to the several great Austrian invasions of 1914. The Allies had taken it for granted that Serbia would be destroyed in a few weeks by the might of the Austrian attack. When the bombardment of Belgrade from across the Sava and Danube began on 29 July, no one expected it to be long before – gallant resistance not withstanding – the Serbs were forced back into the mountains south of their own kingdom. But doubts about Serbia's military prowess were laid to rest during the remaining five months of 1914 by the expulsion of no fewer than three successive 'punitive expeditions' and the capture of 70,000 Austrian prisoners.

Belgrade itself was considered even by the Serbian staff to be incapable of self-defence. Yet, despite the weakness of the forces left to hold the enemy at that point, they were enough to prevent him from crossing the rivers there. The Austrians, startled by the speed of Russian mobilisation, launched their main attack from Bosnia, believing that it was vital for them to advance from these endangered Slav provinces to the west rather than invade frontally from Hungary. This was a strategic error which was to cost the Austrians dearly.

Under Marshal Putnik, whose name is immortalised in the ubiquitous Jugoslav travel agency of the same name, the Serbs routed the Austrians in the first Allied victory of the war. But as the Austrians withdrew, they pursued a scorched earth policy all too familiar in the Second World War but for some surprising in the more formal era of 1914. Women and children were hung or tortured. According to the Red Cross sixty-eight persons had had their eyes gouged out while thirty-four had had their noses cut off.

102

These were the scars left behind in Serbia by the apostles of a superior civilisation.

Such an experience is not easily forgotten, not least as it was repeated on an even more inhumane scale in the Second World War. Violence, never far from the surface in the Balkans, here takes on a particularly brutal aspect which suggests, irrespective of the progress of modern society, that should the walls overlooking the Danube ever resound to conflict again, it will be a particularly bloody experience.

Walking back to the Moskva, the road swept past the Austrian Embassy, still in the same Italianate palace it occupied in 1914, to a small square whose cobbled stones, dilapidated palaces and silent emptiness suggested the flavour of pre-war Belgrade more powerfully than any other street. It is only a few hundred yards from Kalemegdan Park. In the centre of the square there is still a gaping hole, the result, passers-by will explain, of Allied bombing on Easter Sunday in 1944, an event which even today is viewed with considerable suspicion. It was hinted that Marshal Tito might deliberately have persuaded the Allies to bomb the capital on that date knowing that the casualty figures would be high and that public opinion would harden against the British and – so Tito gambled – turn towards the communists. How often Belgrade has suffered at the hands of the reckless and yet how resilient the city has remained. Despite the smog, a choking acrid smell which wakes one at five in the morning most winter days, despite the enormous concentrated concrete bunkers of New Belgrade rising across the Sava, the Serb in Belgrade carries himself with dignity and pride. Sad is the day that has caused this to transpose itself into an altogether more hostile key.

Across the road from the Hotel Moskva, housed in a small glass box of a building, is the best boot-black in the Balkans. A fine oriental-looking gentleman who professes to be of Turkish origin – are not the Serbs, as a French diplomat observed in 1914, only 'poorly baptised Turks'? – shines shoes to a gleam which would not disgrace a guardsman. Unlike most boot-blacks in the Balkans this particular gentleman also makes shoes and was constantly besieged by passers-by to repair leather bags and other articles which he alone, in a street given over to craftsmen of one sort or another, could mend. The small room is pervaded by a powerful smell of glue, and at any moment during the vigorous brushing there is the risk that pots of dye and paint will fall over to ruin everything. Miraculously, this never happens, and with the final application of 'the pleesch', a small velvet cushion, the shoes are ready to excite the admiration of all those who still judge a man's character by the gleam of his boots. In a city which progress and the internal combustion engine have combined to ruin more than any other in Jugoslavia, this man's craft – and let no one imagine the swift transformation of matt leather to mirror-like gleam is not a craft – was a welcome reminder of old-fashioned but undeniably civilised values.

9 ALBANIA IRREDENTA

I was later to learn that however uncivilised Kossovo was said to be the one thing I would not find any shortage of was boot-blacks. Indeed in Prizren I was to come across perhaps one of the most remarkable purveyors of the shiny trade in Europe: Ramadan, a man fluent in six languages (surely a spy! whispered a colleague) who, whatever he lacked in elbow grease, he certainly made up for in entertainment.

Ironically, despite their failure to see eye to eye on many issues, both Serbs and western journalists agree about one thing in Kossovo: its primitive conditions. I have yet to meet a journalist who enjoys visiting what is the most backward part of Jugoslavia. At the same time I have never met a Serb – with the exception of a waiter in Vienna – who believes Kossovo does not represent the nadir of Balkan civilisation.

To reach Priština, the provincial capital, one can take a dull route along the motorway to Niš and then a picturesque tree-lined road into the hills. But those who are prepared to rise early can follow an alternative route favoured by the author on several occasions. At 6.20 a.m. an 'express' train – someone with a sense of humour on the Jugoslav railways has it down in the timetable as a 'business-train' – departs from Belgrade's still faintly Italianate two-storey railway terminus. With a picnic hamper supplied by the courteous and ever helpful staff of the Hotel Moskva, the journey, which takes just over six hours, is relatively painless and remarkably interesting. The line, though single track, was during the war the Axis powers' main route from Central Europe down to Salonika. Crenellated pill-boxes from an even earlier date watch over the line as it winds its way, first past the old palace at Topčider and then through the heart of Serbia to Kragujevac.

Once the line enters Kossovo, towards Mitrovica, the scenery becomes more dramatic. Tall hills rise up on the horizon, and one can enjoy the most spectacular views of castles, now ruined, which before the fateful Battle of Kossovo Field in 1389 defended the Orthodox Church from the incursions of the Turks.

The first time I took this train, a woman of about thirty-five got into my compartment at Kragujevac and we began talking about Kossovo and its problems. But as soon as I tried to raise the issue of Albanian rights I was cut short with the phrase I was to hear so often from the Serbs: '*Kossovo je Serbia!* (Kossovo is Serbian!)' These words, delivered with emphasis, effectively ended any further debate.

Though Priština has a small railway station, this train from Belgrade ends its journey appropriately enough at Kossovo Polje – Kossovo Field, the terrible Field of the Black Birds. Kossovo Polje, apart from a remarkably well-disposed post office which I often had cause to resort to in emergencies, is of little merit. But the great battlefield still circled by sinister black birds, closer to our crows than to blackbirds, remains a poignant spot. On the 600th anniversary of the battle the place was crowded with over a million Serbs who, eager to restore however temporarily the racial balance of the province, poured in from all over Jugoslavia to 'dilute' the ethnic Albanian majority. This ceremony was a crude and, in keeping with most communist celebrations, long-winded affair in which thousands listened in varying degrees of ecstasy to speeches under a scorching sun.

Shut in by a chain of mountains and of vast extent, the plain seems intended by nature for an Armageddon of nations. Around this spot, the Waterloo of Balkan Freedom as it was dubbed in the early years of this century by Englishmen eager to defend those under the Turkish yoke, clusters a whole literature of patriotic ballads from which it is no easy task to discern the true story of that fatal day. 'Armurath', wrote one of the native bards referring to the Turkish hordes, 'had so many men that a horseman could not ride from one wing of his army to the other in a fortnight; the plain of Kossovo was one mass of steel; horse stood against horse, man against man; the spears form a thick forest; the banners obscure the sun, there is no space for a drop of water to fall between them.'

On the other side, Serbs, Bosnians and – though this was carefully concealed at the 600th anniversary – Albanians were forced together in the common cause under the leadership of Prince Lazar. On the morning of 28 June (some historians give the date as 15 June, more appropriate for Waterloo but, sadly, inaccurate) the battle began. Armurath had hesitated to attack the allied host but a dream in which he saw the angel of victory urging him with her laurels to 'annihilate the infidels' inspirited his wavering mind.

The struggle was furious on both sides and Prince Lazar at first held his own against the Ottoman chivalry, but as is usual in Serbian affairs there was a whiff of treachery in the Serbian camp. Vouk Brankovič, to whom one wing of the Serbian army had been entrusted, had long been jealous of his sovereign. It was hinted darkly that he had already agreed with Armurath to betray his master and had been promised the crown of Serbia as a reward. The Turks' victory was the result of this 'great betrayal'. At a critical juncture in the battle when the future of the day was still undecided the traitor turned his horse's head and rode off the field followed by his detachment of 12,000 men.

In vain Lazar attempted to sustain the contest against fearful odds. Relentlessly the Turkish numbers told. Lazar's horse stumbled and fell and there was confusion in the Serbian ranks. Lazar and his nine brothers-in-law along with the flower of the Serbian aristocracy all perished. The victory of the Turks would have been complete but for the death of their own sovereign in the hour of his triumph. According to one legend, Armurath was walking over the battlefield after the fight was over when a wounded Serb, seeing the bright and bejewelled figure of the Sultan, crawled to his feet and pretended to make obeisance to him. Then he suddenly sprang up, drew a dagger from under his garments and plunged it into the victor's breast. The Sultan died and his assassin, Milosh Obilič, was killed after a desperate struggle. Another version of this incident has Milosh being taunted with cowardice by the traitor Vouk on the eve of the battle. To prove his loyalty he went to the Turkish camp and asked to see the Sultan as a deserter, whereupon he smote the Turkish commander to the heart. Whichever version is correct, his name is revered while that of Vouk Brankovič remains despised.

In 1906 an English traveller to the Balkans could write: 'The Battle of Kossovo has never been forgotten in the lands of the southern Slavs. The most mournful songs of Serbian music are inspired by the sad memories of that day. Wherever they have risen against the Turk, the cry of "revenge for Kossovo" has been emblazoned on their banners and the Serbs of Montenegro still wear mourning on their caps for that fateful defeat.' Today the situation has scarcely changed. The Albanians rather than the Turks are now the enemy but Kossovo's power to inflame remains undiminished by the passage of time.

From this melancholy landscape whose memory of sanguinary conflict imparts, as it does across the Adriatic at Lake Trasimene, an undeniably sad spirit, it is only a few dusty miles to Priština. Like rows of jagged broken teeth, the skyscrapers of the provincial capital appear on the horizon through a thick film of dust, like the model city of some 1970s science-fiction serial. Those who know Kossovo only through Priština are understandably perturbed. Epitomising the awful lack of common sense, aesthetic judgement and intelligence which marked the development of the city in the late 1970s stands that least loved of all hotels in the Balkans, the Grand Hotel Priština, as it is named without apparent irony. This crumbling marble skyscraper whose lifts never work and whose bathrooms house innumerable vermin combines the roughness of late nineteenth-century travel with the coldness of twentieth-century hospitality. Behind the long blank desks of the reception resides an impressively bound volume known as the Visitors' Book but used invariably to register complaints. 'Please remove the cockroaches from my bath,' reads the plaintive cry of a Scandinavian visitor. 'There is no plug in my bath,' observes the neat Foreign Office hand of a British consul. Page after page the catalogue of horrors continues while the management adopts an air of Olympian indifference to even the most vociferous objections of its clientele.

From the windows of this building there is little along the skyline to enliven the eye. In all directions rise skyscrapers, thuggish buildings bearing no relation either to the landscape or the populace. There are entire ghettoes here into which during periods of unrest even the most well-armed policeman refuses to venture. One recovers hope however by proceeding along the lime-lined avenue in front of the hotel, which eventually emerges opposite a mosque well over two hundred years old. Here begins the old town, such as it is: barely a couple of streets of private shops and some excellent tailors who will make or mend a pair of trousers at a speed which even the tailors of Hong Kong might envy.

Tempting though it is to idealise the Albanians and contrast them favourably with the Serbs, they remain essentially inscrutable. The young Albanian men with their round, dark faces, flatter than the Serbs and with less angular noses, appear so open towards the western traveller that he usually fails to detect that dark menace in the eye which is so apparent to the Serb and which for centuries made the Albanians the most feared and warlike race in the Balkans. In Constantinople, the Sultan's bodyguard was Albanian; indeed Albanian regiments enjoyed under the Sultan the kind of formidable reputation Highlanders have in the British army. As Leslie Gardiner has written in *The Eagle Spreads his Claws*, 'The history of Albania is one long chapter of misery and revolt, subjection and savagery. Her songs are all martial songs, her poems and legends all fighting talk, her great men – Pyrrhus, Alexander the Great, Skanderbeg and Kemal Ataturk all warlike men who rose to command empires but never managed to unify their native land.'

When Edward Lear toured Albania, he was pelted with mud for gathering watercress at a stream, stoned for wearing a white hat and nearly lynched for sketching a medieval ruin. In one place he saw dogs playing with a human head in the bazaar. And all this was long before anyone had heard of communism. What particularly put Lear off parts of Albania was the seclusion of the place. The Serbs allege today that the Albanians remain untrustworthy and filthy, impervious to the 'benefits' of modern society. Of untrustworthiness, the western traveller finds little, but once he passes the old town mosque in Priština, the old-fashioned squalor asserts itself everywhere. Past a shop selling Albanian wedding dresses, richly embroidered waistcoats and pillbox hats, a small café remains popular with the few Serbs who live in the city. 'They're all crooks!' an elderly Serb lady leant across from her table to exclaim. 'All crooks and dirty. Everywhere ... everywhere', she repeated with passion, pointing at a pile of tins and rotting fruit and vegetables deposited opposite between the lofty Lombardy poplars.

The trees had been planted by the Italians who moved swiftly into Albania during the last war when the German blitzkrieg struck the north of Jugoslavia. These wonderful trees and the old railway station built of Istrian stone are the only remnants of their brief stay. With characteristic adaptability, most of the Albanian shopkeepers here have simply erected their shops around the trees, so that it is not uncommon to walk into a shop selling the ubiquitous wedding dresses and find half the available space taken up by a vast tree trunk rising through a hole in the roof. This gentle solution to a problem solved more ruthlessly in northern Europe is endearing; tree, merchandise and shopkeeper are none the worse for the compromise.

These minor diversions aside, there is little to delay one in Priština. As relations between Serbs and Albanians deteriorated, a tension which nourished sullenness and suspicion made itself felt. In 1989, when the Albanians declared strikes in protest at Belgrade stripping them of their autonomy, to enter a Serbian shop was to encounter a palpable sensation of fear. However much they despise the Albanians, the Serbs here know that if the Albanians were so minded they could all be massacred within hours. Such thoughts are hardly conducive to trust or to calm. Later that year, after more than thirty ethnic Albanians had been shot by the security forces, the atmosphere deteriorated even further, leaving as it does today a reluctance to linger even in the more picturesque parts of the province.

A young Albanian medical student who spent his spare time in a shop selling colourful velvet hair slides explained with the logical detachment of a western European intellectual the prospects for the province. 'It's quite straightforward,' he said, drawing a chart with a pencil. 'By the year 1995 we will be the most populous people in Jugoslavia, and by the year 2110 numerically the most powerful people in the entire Balkan peninsula. So you see time is on *our* side, *not* Belgrade's.'

From Priština it is a little over an hour in a fast car – and the Albanians drive very fast – to the most lovely city in the entire province and one whose charm can compare with any settlement in inland Jugoslavia. Prizren, cradle of both Serbian and Albanian cultures, where the first Albanian newspaper was printed and the first Albanian language broadcast was heard, is a place which lingers in the memory. To reach it one travels across some of the most attractive countryside in the Balkans: up forest-clad hills where the finest spring water can still be drunk with impunity; down winding roads across field after field of gentle crops, all beneath the gaze of snow-capped peaks stretching far and wide across every horizon.

The city itself is approached along a narrow tree-lined avenue of houses, all Italianate stucco with first-floor balconies. The ground floor of each of these is a shop selling yet more Albanian wedding costumes, or domestic utensils like the delightful brass Albanian teapots of singular design. By far the most interesting of these shops is to be found on the corner before the Therandra Hotel. Here, imbued with the loving expertise of centuries of tradition, is the maker of that most picturesque item of Balkan headgear, the Albanian *plish*. This white egg-cup hat is worn by every Albanian man irrespective of age or rank, except for those teenagers who see it as incompatible with their leather jackets and blue jeans. The hat varies in shape and size depending on the region of Albania. In Kossovo, especially around Priština, it is generally low and broad. In the hills it is higher and more pointed. In the Albanian state itself it is the same shape as a fez, i.e. square, and much less picturesque.

In the Prizren *plish* shop, great care was taken to ensure that only the finest wool was employed. This wool once spun was moulded on a wooden head roughly the shape of half a rugby ball, then soaked and dried time and again until it stiffened into a perfectly effective item of headdress. The entire process takes the best part of six weeks. The shop was small and dark, comprising only two rooms: a showroom and a workshop. While a wizened old man worked feverishly in the latter, the former had the air of reverential silence once to be associated with a good hatter in St James. There were no queues, no crowds, no loud or pointed questions and yet the showroom was always full.

Sometimes a whole transaction was conducted in silence. One fine figure of a man came in, took off his own *plish* – a dark grey and sweat-soiled brown number – rested it on the table and gazed into the shopkeeper's face with a look of gentle inquiry. After gazing at the venerable object for a few seconds, the shopkeeper gave a professional shrug of his shoulders, grimaced and shook his head. The disappointed customer looked utterly crestfallen, turned on his heel and was gone. 'We often have requests to repair the *plish*,' the shopkeeper explained. 'Usually we can refurbish them, rewash and stiffen but ... you saw; this man's *plish* must have belonged to his grandfather.'

Time and again around the small back streets of Prizren I was struck by a sight which more than anything else conjured up visions of Aubrey Herbert's 'dignified bandit' and Edith Durham's 'high

Albanian'. This was the appearance, never more than two at any time, of splendid octogenarian men, still six foot tall with backs straight as ramrods and fine waxed moustaches. Their weather-beaten but finely chiselled profiles made them look like Indian Army officers back for a reunion on the Khyber. If one had dressed them in English uniform I doubt whether even a Guards colour sergeant would have questioned their credentials. So English in fact did they look that on more than one occasion I approached one of these Osbert Lancaster-like characters optimistically thinking that they might understand English. None did.

Their bearing and dignity was of a kind which I did not see when visiting Albania and clearly no longer exists in Mr Hoxha's unfortunate creation. Their survival suggested that the old patri-archal system of society was still preserved here in Prizren. These men were clearly used to command. Perhaps twenty-five years ago they had enjoyed the right of life or death over miscreants in the family, dispensing justice and acting like God. Edward Lear remarked during his travels in Albania how similar to the Scottish Highlanders the people here were. Both were fiercely proud, both were ruled by chieftains and both surrounded themselves with customs impenetrable to the foreigner.

Will such figures die out by the end of this century? Months later on a train between Priština and Prizren I found myself sitting opposite one of these patriarchs, his eyes twinkling, his fine chin resting on his stick. Conversation even on a most elementary level was beyond him and despite the benign eyes I noted with a slight shudder that his large hands were covered in blood stains. 'He had to kill a pig,' the man's grandson explained reassuringly. The grandson, a small, slight man barely five feet six, would hardly have passed for a blood relative. He was an intellectual, fluent in English and highly politicised but physically he bore witness to the break-down in the patrician tradition which Kossovo, for all its back-wardness, was also experiencing.

The only hotel in Prizren, the Therandra, is a modest four-storey building which like the Grand in Priština, leaves a lot to be desired but compensates in part for this by offering fabulous views across mosques, crumbling buildings and hills towards the Albanian fron-tier. In some of the rooms parts of the wall are engagingly missing, revealing the intricacies of 1960s brickwork. In other rooms the

furniture appears in that broken state which recalls a college combination room after a rugby dinner. But the place is clean and
beneath it gurgles the age-old spring of Therandra. At dawn the
anguished cry of the muezzin rises above the city from a handful
of pretty mosques.

Across the road from the hotel runs a fast-flowing stream beyond
which clusters a series of wonderful buildings in varying stages of
dilapidation. To the right, behind a small square, a picturesque
tree-lined road runs up to the Catholic church. To the left, more
informal cobbled streets lead to a pretty yellow stucco inn and
nearby a pleasant café with views – when the clouds clear – of the
peaks between Albania and Montenegro.

Above the city on a small eminence is the church of St Saviour
dating from the fourteenth century. Below is the more attractive
St Nicholas which escaped destruction by the Turks thanks to a
noteworthy trick. Its congregation covered it with earth and rubble
so that the Turks did not recognise it as a church at all. Even today
when its covering of earth has long disappeared, it faintly resembles
a cave, and even on the hottest day in August is invariably dark
and cold.

In the days of its medieval greatness under Tsar Dushan when
Prizren was the proud capital of a Serbian empire, there were 360
churches and monasteries. We can get some idea of this opulence
in the remarkable church behind the Therandra Hotel dedicated to
the Mother of God which has magnificent thirteenth-century fres-
coes depicting Christ's miracles. But the church of St Peter is
perhaps the most extraordinary of all, for here legend narrates a
most splendid miracle which to this day every inhabitant of Prizren
recalls.

When the Turks first came to Prizren after the Battle of Kossovo
Field, a great concourse of people gathered in the church of St Peter
to pray for protection against the Infidel. It must have seemed to
them that God did not hear them for the Turks fell upon them and
massacred them all, men, women and children, flinging their bodies
to the dogs in the courtyard. And yet, proclaimed the bearded priest
who showed us around, God did show his hand on that terrible
day. For the Turks, satiated with murder, turned to looting. They
particularly coveted the great gilded crosses on the altar – though
these were only gilt they looked like gold. But as the first man laid

his hand upon them he fell down dead; another followed, and he, too, dropped in his steps. Yet another; and then the Turks saw that a miracle was upon them and they fled in terror from the church.

So powerful was their fear that while almost all the other churches of Prizren were ravaged and destroyed during the long Turkish occupation, St Peter's survived largely intact. The priest will usually point out where the Turks fell, a black spot on the stone floor. This was a miracle – a *first-class* miracle, he claims. Even today it appears no idle story, for the gilt crosses are on the altar for all to see.

So much for the Serbian remains, although older Serbs in Prizren will recount the desperate story of their nation's heroic retreat in the First World War through Prizren and across the Albanian mountains to the sea. During this retreat 100,000, the flower of the Serbian nation, perished in the coldest winter the Balkan peninsula had recorded for two centuries. The brave remnants of the Serbian army which finally collected on the Adriatic coast to be rescued by English warships numbered barely a few thousand souls.

Not far from the Sinan Pasha mosque, whose minaret rises high above some pollarded limes, is the small wooden headquarters of the Prizren League, a doll's house of Albanian nationalism where the weapons, ceremonial swords and uniforms of the Albanians who fought against the Turks are preserved. There are now fine old sepia photographs of the first Albanian ministers sent to parley with the Sultan in a room dark with musty fabrics which look as if they have not been changed for more than a hundred years. In another room devoted to more modern times there are a number of contemporary paintings recalling the heroic uprising of Skanderbeg. One canvas in particular depicting thousands of white-fezzed Albanian warriors struck me as particularly chilling. Here in oil was the Serbs' nightmare.

Back outside the Therandra Hotel, Ramadan, boot-black by profession, jester by inclination and most probably spy by upbringing kept up a steady flow of witty responses to all political questions, deftly avoiding a compromising comment here, neatly side-stepping an argument there. 'Today we have problems,' he began with a twinkle in his eye before reciting – and each time it was a different theme – 'Today we have twenty banks in Prizren but no money.

Four hospitals, no doctors. Thousands of mothers and no children,'
etc. He had learnt Italian under the occupation and seemed at home
with all his customers, irrespective of race or political persuasion,
commenting with professional pride on the different ethnic costumes
of the inhabitants who passed picturesquely in front of us every
minute. There were enormous ladies wearing striped dresses with a
wooden plank suspended across the hips to help them carry bundles
of washing. These were, Ramadan explained, Albanians from close
to the frontier. Then there were tall ladies with white headscarves;
'Serbian Christians – very traditional', he observed. Finally, as well
as the Albanians with their *plishes*, there were countless Turks
wearing pantaloons.

Less colourful was the sight nearby of the first Jugoslav army
tank. Following the incorporation of Kossovo into Serbia, an event
accompanied by much celebration and fireworks in Belgrade, the
military, the only federal organisation left with any authority,
patrolled up and down the province to discourage any public protest
on the part of the Albanians. Travelling across the country one got
used to seeing Jugoslav tanks, sometimes in convoys fifty strong,
rumbling up and down the hills. Fortunately for them, no one was
going to ask them to get involved should the Albanians cut up
rough. This disagreeable task fell to the lot of the paramilitary riot
police, and indeed it was they who opened fire on 30 March 1989
in Dečane, killing several Albanian demonstrators in a brief and
bloody exchange.

As we entered Dečane, a town renowned until then more for its
superb Orthodox monastery than for any insurrection, a fifteen-
strong convoy of ambulance vehicles passed us on the road for Peč.
Along the main village street police pickets were being established.
As usual the change of the guard was sloppy and by very good
luck – that most treasured friend of any foreign correspondent –
we managed to slip in unnoticed between shifts. At a café, small
groups of Albanians stood around with blank expressions on their
faces. Broken glass, rubble and a semi-demolished lamppost all
showed evidence of a struggle. A nervous furtive man sidled up and
offered to tell us something of the struggle if we joined him in
another café. But as soon as we started talking, the ears of two
plain-clothes policemen in a corner visibly pricked up and he
stopped. 'Later,' he whispered, 'follow me.' This we attempted to

115

do as inconspicuously as is possible in a town in which all eyes appear focused on anyone who moves. But as the two plain-clothes policemen also followed the exercise was abandoned.

Outside the Café Park, whose window sported a series of bullet-holes that would do justice to a saloon bar in any Western, I scoured the ground for a few minutes searching for what I'm sure the authorities had gone to great lengths to sweep away. With delight I found under a car a couple of Kalashnikov cartridge cases, which Albanian doctors were later to claim had been primed with soft-nosed dum-dum bullets. This was unlikely but without doubt the authorities' fire-discipline had been very poor and casualties were much higher than the official tally of twenty-four dead. Sadly, 30 March 1989 will never be forgotten by the Albanians.

In Peč, where another magnificent Serbian Orthodox monastery offers probably the most spectacular frescos in Kossovo, the atmosphere was more relaxed. But even here the westerner who engaged a local in conversation soon discovered the depth of outrage felt by the Albanians. 'Every day we lose two or three men from beatings,' said an umbrella-maker who had learned his trade from the Italians. At a nearby barber's, the message from a teenage apprentice who spoke fluent English was the same: 'We are treated so badly. We will never find jobs. We can only emigrate. It is our only chance.' Suddenly this gangly young boy with a pale spotty countenance said, 'Quick, come with me,' and I was propelled by the arm into a barber's chair and confronted with a six-inch razor of the type our grandfathers called a 'safety' model. Two deft strokes and a small piece of stubble I had overlooked in the darkened bathroom of the Therandra was dispatched.

In Kossovo, where the razor and the barber are still a daily part of most people's lives, there is perhaps no better way to tap the pulse of what the local people think than to expose oneself to the sure hands of the Albanian barber. In Prizren most of the barbers are Turkish, immaculately courteous gentlemen whose shops boast brass basins and fittings and giant tin shaving bowls. Some rather alarmingly have only one eye. Others, more worryingly still, twitch incessantly. All however possess that generosity of spirit which underlines the present crisis in Kossovo as a tragedy for the Balkans as well as for Jugoslavia. A combination of gentle hospitality and violence however is nothing new in this part of the world. As Robert

Curzon said during his tour of the great monasteries of the Levant at the end of the last century: 'I have been quietly dining in a monastery and shots have been heard.'

10 A FRIEND OF BULGARIA

The great monasteries of the Levant which Robert Curzon visited have survived in Bulgaria only as tourist attractions. Communism has little time for spiritual diversions it cannot control. One advantage of this, however, is that unlike Curzon and later travellers to the monasteries of Bulgaria, it is no longer necessary to climb up rope-ladders to gain admittance to what were virtual fortresses. J. D. Bourchier (1850–1920), *The Times'* first and greatest correspondent in the Balkans, left a vivid description of his ascent into a Balkan monastery. 'Windlass to bottom seems almost 300 feet but precipice descends on either side of causeway much lower – monks let down top swinging ladder (in joists) – sensation of getting from one to other not pleasant – rungs loose – ladder swings out – I pause to disentangle coat pocket caught in the end of one of the rungs ...'

Of all the Englishmen and women who opened their hearts to the Bulgarians – they include such diverse figures as Gladstone and Lady Strangford – Bourchier remains the most picturesque. This former Eton schoolmaster, described by one of his pupils as 'unmistakeably and obviously a gentleman with a keen sense of honour and free from all pretentiousness and uneasy suspicions', was also perhaps the most extraordinary. 'That is the man', wrote another of his former charges at Eton, 'whose word controlled the destinies of nations and the guns of three continental armies; and that is the master in whom we saw nothing but inability or unwillingness to force us through the round of school routine. We do not come very well out of it.'

After dinner with another old Etonian, *The Times'* correspondent in Vienna, Mr Brinsley Richards, Bourchier repaired to the island of Lussin Piccolo in the Quarnero to muse on the future. He had been forced on account of increasing deafness to give up being a beak at Eton. Literary ambition and an inquiring mind, classically trained, inevitably set him thinking about *The Times*, then a more leisurely paper than today. Richards had been impressed when they met in Vienna, and on hearing of an uprising in Romania telegrammed Bourchier to make all haste to the Romanian capital and then to Bulgaria, also said to be in a state of considerable unrest.

What followed has been echoed time and again by later *Times* foreign correspondents setting out on their first mission, and foolish is the editor who writes a man off just because his early efforts end unsuccessfully. Accepting Richards' proposal, Bourchier looked about for a steamer to convey him from his island to Fiume, but found there was none for several days. He accordingly chartered a sailing boat to the mainland where he found a steamer. But eight days later he had only reached Vienna. Richards, unamused by this tardiness, coolly informed him that since the peasants in Bulgaria had been so disobliging as to allow their rising to be suppressed, Bourchier had come too late. At this point only the most tenacious would have proceeded but Bourchier was an Irishman and a most engaging one to boot. Lady Grogan, his biographer, relates in a paragraph memorable for its understatement that 'with the assistance of Mrs Richards, an extremely charming and gifted woman, Bourchier finally induced Richards to relent and allow him to proceed to Romania'.

Thus came about one of the most remarkable episodes in *The Times'* foreign correspondence and a footnote to Balkan history. In frequent contact with the crowned heads of the Balkans, particularly King Ferdinand of Bulgaria, and capable of sustaining himself on a diet of oil and anchovies month in month out, Bourchier became an inescapable figure on the Balkan scene. He went native, in the tradition of many *Times* foreign correspondents – he even dressed like a native. He remained, however, notoriously chaotic and prone to extravagant bouts of unpunctuality. His diary is full of phrases such as 'Mislaid keys – lost entire afternoon searching for them.'

But however often he forgot to turn up for dinner, however frequently he was late, time and again his counsel was sought for he had the ear of all the principal players in the Balkan game. London predictably took a less charitable line over Bourchier's mercurial temperament. While Mackenzie Wallace was head of the newspaper's Foreign Department, Bourchier's relations with the office were tranquil. But, as is so often the case, a change of personnel soon unsettled this calm. The new head of the Foreign Department, Valentine Chirol, found Bourchier personally unsympathetic. In April 1907 Chirol drew Bourchier's attention to the fact that by delaying an article reviewing the causes of an uprising in Moldavia he had compromised *The Times*, which had had to suffer the humiliation of being forestalled by the *Morning Post*.

As always finances, never generous, also contributed to Bourchier's fall from favour. The manager, it was widely agreed, knowing himself to be forced to keep the journalists' expenses as low as possible had come to dread the arrival of Bourchier's 'lectures' on Crete, wired at five shillings per word instead of being posted for only tuppence ha'penny and only 'explaining the insignificant details of a rumpus in one small Turkish island'. In a finely tuned piece of sarcasm once so frequently encountered among London managers and editors but now rather rare, Moberley Bell the manager pulled out his tables and clearly relished the chance of exploiting Bourchier's chronic inability to count: 'An average copy of *The Times* contains about 160,000 words and if you send us 1,400 words on Crete you are proposing to take up 1/115th of our space for that insignificant island whose entire population is only 1/136th of even the British Isles and 1/540th of the British Empire ... These mathematical calculations will, I know, be insuperably difficult for your Cambridge mind, but the net result may be intelligible – we really *must* have shorter telegrammes.'

Like many a *Times* foreign correspondent, Bourchier was to end his days in exile. Appropriately enough he found the monastery at Rila, a day's drive south of Sofia, which combines the characteristics of a fortress and a religious retreat, the most suitable place for his end. Today his grave still stands some 5,000 feet above the sea, surrounded by lofty mountains which form a spur of the Rhodope range and which include some of the highest summits in the Balkan peninsula..

The monastery of Rila has been the focus in Bulgaria not only of the national religion but also of patriotic sentiment. Its history is interwoven with that of Christianity in the Balkans; it is to Bulgaria what Mont St Michel is to Normandy or the Grand Chartreuse to Dauphiné. For centuries it kept alive the light of the faith in the heart of the peninsula, though so many of its neighbours embraced the creed of Islam. In the early years of this century it formed a link both political and religious between the Free Bulgarians and their not forgotten brethren in Macedonia.

Its founder was St Ivan Rilski, the St Bruno of Bulgaria, who was born in 876. For years this holy man had wandered over the mountains seeking a spot where he might find a pious retreat; at one time he lived in a hollow tree, at another in a cave among the rocks. At length he fixed his dwelling in the mountains above the present site of the monastery. There his fame for exorcising demons and treating incurable maladies brought disciples to his side and the little band constructed a chapel and some rude dwellings; the chapel still exists and there is a grotto nearby into which pilgrims descend through a chimney-like passage cut in the rock. Here the saint was buried but his bones were afterwards removed to Sofia where they have remained for five hundred years.

When Bourchier first arrived there in 1890, Prince Ferdinand, the heir to the Bulgarian throne, was staying in the monastery. It was then garrisoned by two companies of infantry, besides a force of gendarmes and a cavalry escort. Its cloistered quadrangles were crowded with soldiers in their white summer uniforms, dark-robed monks and picturesquely clad peasants making their annual pilgrimages to the shrine. Today such colour is absent, sadly, though the mountains and the monastery are still covered with magnificent primeval forests, chiefly of beech and pine. Many of the trees attain an enormous size and bears and wolves are by no means unknown here. But step inside Rila these days and the atmosphere is very remote from that which Bourchier encountered.

Throughout Bulgaria, children are encouraged to behave with reverence towards communist shrines. In every town there is some fearsome concrete sculpture invariably crowned by a red star, which schoolchildren are taken to visit each month. They stand silent and anxious, staring with studied concentration at blocks of abstract art too hideous to describe. At Rila, however, the church might have been a playground. The children there were not struck by the gorgeous interior which equals if it does not surpass anything of the kind to be seen at Mount Athos. Every inch of the walls and vaulted ceiling is covered with frescos; there is a magnificent gilded iconostasis in front of which once reposed the hand and arm of St

Ivan Rilski. The north wall in particular is covered with an immense picture of the Day of Judgement. At the top sits God the Father with Christ and the Virgin Mary; a stream of fire issues from the feet and falls into Hell, which is represented here as elsewhere by a fish with a great yawning mouth and terrible teeth. To the right, groups of saints standing on small clouds sail through the air. These and other glories seem to leave the young communists of Bulgaria cold.

The monastic community, now shrunk to barely a tenth of the size it was when Bourchier was laid to rest there, is conspicuous only by its absence, though official visitors will be royally entertained in the building by impressive bearded abbots who politely refuse to discuss political questions except to say how marvellously they are looked after by the communists.

In one respect, however, nothing has changed since Bourchier's day. The Bulgarians are still persecuting Turks on Bulgarian soil. Last year, following an earlier policy of assimilation and enforced name-changing, tens of thousands of Turks fled across the frontier to Turkey. This despite the publicity it attracted is nothing new. Indeed in 1895 *The Times*, believing its honour to be at stake on account of Bourchier's angrily denied dispatches, went so far as to defray the expenses of an investigation into the general charge of persecution of Turks on Bulgarian soil. Bourchier himself entered a Turkish village called Dospat to find what he called a 'Terrible scene. Resembled Sodom and Gomorrah after Fire and Brimstone. Crowds of villagers ... Slept in a house of a fanatical mullah with revolver by pillow.'

Over a hundred years later, the scenes were less violent but bitter enough to see that generations on, Bulgarian attitudes towards the Turks remained hostile and intolerant. 'Of course they are paying off old scores. But we of course have never made a rumpus about it because we never had any copper-bottomed proof,' was the cool response of a senior British diplomat early in 1988. It took the combined attack of the British press and Armenian and Turkish protest for this view to change. By late 1989 Bulgaria was being hauled over the coals by everyone for her treatment of the Turks. Bulgarian ministers told bemused journalists that homogeneity was of vital interest to the country. These people were not Turks anyway, they were Bulgars. Sofia really did want them to remain, but was it so unreasonable to ask them to be good Bulgars and give up their 'assumed' Turkish names?

Visits to the affected areas were illuminating. At first they were carefully monitored, but later they were ignored as the Bulgarians resigned themselves to western opprobrium. How similar these scenes were to those in Kossovo. The same winning sympathy extended to the western visitor. The same pleas for help. The same long and weary tales of atrocities and violence. Like the Tibetans after the Chinese invasion these Turks voted with their feet and just left in their tens of thousands.

Though the exodus inflicted considerable economic damage on the Bulgarians, there was no indication that except in official circles dealing with the foreign press there would be any remorse of a lasting nature. For the Turks who remain, however, and there are now about 300,000, there is little optimism. A few miles from the Turkish frontier I met an old and hospitable man in his sixties who said he would never leave. 'My family has been here for six hundred years. They have taken my children away and they insist that I do not worship in the mosques and of course I am called Boris, no longer Mehmet – but still I shall stay,' he said, rising to his feet with a look of philosophical resignation.

These scenes so familiar to the experienced Balkan traveller should not prevent the visitor enjoying in Sofia, as he has in Belgrade, the attractions of a capital still remarkably free from the stresses of western urban life. In Sofia no one, it is clear from the very moment one leaves the railway station, is ever in a hurry. From the sparkling marble foyer of the Hotel Balkan Sheraton to the long avenue of quaint houses which runs past the Dmitroff shrine to the town museum, the pace is slow even in winter.

Dmitroff, it may be recalled, was accused of setting the Reichstag on fire and found guilty by the Nazis. His tomb like Lenin's is a darkened sombre shrine which the amusing Syldavian uniforms of the guards do little to invest with humour. As usual it is an audience of children who predominate. Most, however, seemed more intrigued by the scarlet and white uniforms of the guards than by the grim corpse within.

Nearby is the National Gallery, housed in a fine old villa whose wooden staircases surely resounded to Bourchier's wit as it once, judging by the escutcheon near the door, belonged to the Coburgs –

the family which 'supplied' Prince Ferdinand. This peaceful haven of old Balkan bourgeois values is invariably deserted save for the deputy curator whose long fingers, smiling eyes and flashing teeth restore one's faith in the quality of the Bulgarian woman.

Up a final flight of wooden stairs an old keeper, erect and with bright blue eyes, confides that his father was once a retainer in the villa and that in his own way, communism notwithstanding, he is continuing the family tradition. To the right opens up a room full of blue pastelly portraits of exotic women in languid poses. Between the wars Sofia, like so many Balkan cities, was a more racy place than it has ever been since. Some of the artists had clearly studied in Paris and many more married their own vision of life to a technique which would not have disgraced a more western salon. Bencho Obreshokov's portrait of a lady shows this successful cross-fertilisation of cultures most memorably, although the giant Slav lady of the earlier Ivan Nenov painting appears to be a more lasting appraisal of the traditional Bulgarian look. What all these artists capture is the glorious mellow light of the Balkan winter when the sun filters through dust and mist, highlighting at every corner the fine details of first one and then another building.

Sadly, Sofia, like Belgrade, has suffered the ravages of modern planning and there is little to keep the visitor in this city for long. Better that he should discover the remains of Philipopolis on the Black Sea or strike inland to the magnificent pine-clad hills of Rila. Most western visitors to Bulgaria are businessmen, however, who tend to do neither, heading off instead to discover the delights of one of the prettiest parts of the country, the small town of Plovdiv where each spring a trade fair – the biggest in the Balkans – takes place.

Plovdiv itself shows traces of Armenian culture. The old town's houses represent some of the most exquisite examples of wooden-carved architecture to be found anywhere in Europe. In one, a kind of town museum called the old merchant's house, a thin, strikingly oriental-looking woman of about thirty guided us through a series of rooms whose carved decoration might have impressed Grinling Gibbons. This was all, our minder informed us, *Bulgarian* art, but it was clear both from the demeanour of the curator and the strange delicacy of all we saw that this building owed much to the Armenian rather than the Slav Bulgarian culture. Unlike the Turks the Armen-

125

ians had quietly assimilated, turning a blind eye to such tours as ours which ignored their very existence.

The fair itself is like most trade fairs noisy, crowded and ultimately dissatisfying for visitors and exhibitors alike. Threading my way through a crowd of excited East Germans admiring the latest computer creation from Hungary, I was startled to see on a large board the well-known name of a distinguished wine merchant close to St James's Palace. Behind the board sat the only Englishman apart from myself I could find in this 'international fair'. Peering at me through a pair of half-moons, his enormous frame held together by red braces, this middle-aged gentleman regarded me with suspicion tinged with dismay as if someone had caught him in a place in which he was really not supposed to be. The ice broken by a few words which indicated that we were not in competition for any potential claret drinkers in the Balkans, he proceeded to give a thumbnail sketch of Balkan alcoholic beverages. The spirits were all 'filthy', the beer undrinkable, and the Black Sea Bulgarian wines? 'Reasonable plonk,' he grudgingly conceded, suggesting that Bulgaria and even Plovdiv for all its charms was a dull posting for a man used to greater things.

It was at Plovdiv that I first noticed the unwelcome attentions of the Bulgarian security service who then regarded all foreign correspondents as spies and generally conspired to ensure that one was not left alone for longer than a second. It was reassuring to read that Bourchier had run into this problem as well. During a visit to the interior in 1888 his movements were watched day and night, a gendarme being attached to him who kept vigil beneath his window throughout the night. During an Orthodox Easter Service which lasted several hours, the gendarme, 'posting himself on my left hand, proceeded to inflict upon me at intervals a series of nudges by way of reminder that he had not forgotten me'. The occasion for this vigilance it later transpired was that Bourchier had telegraphed *en clair* to Bucharest for a revolver which he had left there, fuelling Bulgarian suspicions that he was an assassin.

These days the surveillance is less crude and intimate, though just as irritating. Admiring the remains of a fine Roman amphitheatre in Plovdiv, I looked up to see a thin, angular young man with mirror glasses and a dark suit staring down at me. This man was later to crop up in other corners of the city and even to reappear

126

in Sofia where my opportunity to lose him provoked the most memorable rebuke of the tour. 'Next time, Bassett,' intoned a large lady representing the Sofia press, 'it will be umbrella'; a not too subtle allusion to the ill-fated Bulgarian *émigré* Markov murdered with a poisonous umbrella as he strolled nonchalantly across the Thames one morning.

Bulgaria, lying as it does at the heart of the Balkan peninsula, has long enjoyed a reputation for dark dealing which Markov's murder, the attempted assassination of the Pope and murky goings-on with gun-runners have long reinforced. The Bulgarian authorities are keen to refute this at sometimes tiresome length. Until recently nearly every western correspondent arriving in Sofia was subjected at some stage to an interminable speech about the West's 'flawed perception' of Bulgaria, and yet its dark reputation lives on. It is almost as if the name was sufficient in itself to cause any God-fearing man to tremble upon arrival in the country. As Bourchier knew all too well, assassination is nothing new for the Bulgarians. One of his earliest dispatches for *The Times* concerned the dramatic attack on the Chief Minister, Stambolov, who 'received over twenty wounds on the head. Both hands which he raised to protect himself were almost cut off.' The head of *The Times* Foreign Department minuted grimly to Bourchier, 'As a spirit of political assassination seems to be abroad in Bulgaria, it might be well if you sent us a biography of Prince Ferdinand. I sincerely trust it may lie in our pigeon-hole for many years, but it is well to be prepared for all emergencies.'

Perhaps it is unfair to come down hard on the Bulgarians. They have in decades progressed enormously from the most backward of all people in the peninsula to a nation whose dignity and respect for the past are, despite years of communism, preserved intact. In Warsaw, where the Bulgarian Embassy occupies a palatial establishment between the Swiss and Mongolian embassies, the gentleman responsible for dealing with foreign correspondents was a grey-haired man whose demeanour and powerful build itself suggested long service in the Balkan Wars. I shall never forget how, on bidding me to sit down, he asked me of Gladstone and then proceeded, gazing with lost eyes at a peeling stucco ceiling, to talk to himself about Gladstone and 1878. In most embassies the press attaché, or information officer as he is sometimes ironically called these days, is a youth enjoying his first posting. In this Bulgarian embassy it seemed as if the most elderly and senior man in the service had been chosen for a distant posting dealing with a western press corps numbering barely eight souls.

The Bulgarians do not discard their old-fashioned values lightly. *Perestroika* and *glasnost* have certainly made the country more relaxed, but despite mild revolution, the country's progress is inhibited by the enormous backwardness of the prevailing political. environment. Nothing appeared to underline this more than the rigid schooling in which short haircuts, uniforms and total obedience were the prerequisites of early education. The western 'vices' of drugs and pop music were banished so that the disciplined ideology of the party retained total control. This may partly explain the remarkably docile behaviour of nearly every young person I met in Bulgaria. Some manifested a slight interest in football. Others also expressed curiosity about the latest trends in rock music. But by far the majority expressed remarkably little interest in the West and indeed in the progress of *glasnost* in Moscow. Quiet, self-sufficient, these inheritors of the heartland of the Balkans are still made of the same stoic stuff Bourchier knew. Thanks to their ability just to rub along, Bulgars have had few of the dissident problems besetting other communist countries. The opposition was until recently only a cypher. Food and wine are plentiful and the usual intellectuals' complaints aside, most people seem happy to follow the path communism has organised for them. Compared to Jugo-slavia to the west and Romania in the north, the degree of stability is indeed enviable. So far *perestroika* has taken a more peaceful path than anything in either of those lands.

Back in the Hotel Balkan Sheraton, a small group of Bulgar businessmen – with western suits and briefcases but old-fashioned courtesy – discussed the future of the country. Would the Sheraton group which had invested in the once extravagantly seedy Hotel Balkan – a well-known brothel for Arabs – but now the flagship of hotels in Eastern Europe, pull out? When would the communists really permit market forces in the western sense to take over? These and other such questions still await some characteristically Bulgarian resolution, of a type which would have been close to Bourchier's heart.

11 LIGHTS OUT IN BUCHAREST

With a feeling of trepidation and no little excitement, I peered out of the aircraft window as it lost height on its approach to Bucharest. It was the spring of 1986 when I had last visited the Romanian capital, then in the grip of one of the most appalling dictatorships in the history of the post-war world. Then, it had been necessary to disguise any journalistic activity by resorting to almost pantomime extremes. My visa stated that I was a 'harpist', not a foreign correspondent. Too many reporters had been allowed in only to be followed relentlessly by the hated Securitate secret police. There was no foolproof way of pulling the wool over these thugs' eyes but on the grounds of nothing ventured nothing gained an attempt had to be made.

There were few more sinister airports in Europe to land at than Bucharest. The evening flight from Budapest – after climbing over the Transylvanian peaks with a breathtaking glimpse of the sun setting over the distant Tatras on the horizon – appears to drop out of the sky to a totally deserted landscape. In vain the eye searched for the landing lights of an international airport or the friendly urban glow of a great city. Below there was only darkness; cold, unwelcoming, even menacing. With fuel cuts and electricity rationing the winter of 1986 had been no different from that of the previous two years. Austerity was the order of the day and it began almost before one had even left the aeroplane.

At the airport terminal fur-coated soldiers blew on their hands to keep warm. A cursory inspection of luggage was followed by a long queue to exchange money in a darkness unrelieved save by oil lamps. Most exhausting of all was a prolonged examination of one's 'data' by a computer, old and cumbersome but nonetheless effective. I assume it was effective, for on receiving my details a curious look spread over the officer's face and he stared hard at the document as if unsure what to do. After a few minutes he smiled politely, excused himself and left the box for a few minutes to return with a plain-clothes gentleman to whom he pointed me out, rather too conspicuously I felt. The plain-clothes man gave the same polite smile and moved off into the shadows. After a minute my passport was stamped and I was free to proceed to the nearest taxi rank where lounged half a dozen men, all in heavy woollen coats.

One claimed he was a taxi driver but I imagined he was probably a policeman, though that did not stop him exchanging my packet of Kent cigarettes for 50 lei, the equivalent of £30 sterling at the official rate.

Having read, like most Balkan buffs, the lengthy Balkan trilogy of Olivia Manning's, I had convinced myself that the only hotel I could possibly stay at was the illustrious Athenée Palace on the Calea Victoreiae opposite the former royal palace. There are no doubt many who would dispute the charms of this once great establishment but in the conditions of the Ceausescu 'golden era' then prevailing in Romania, I had no reason to believe that there was any other hotel which could match the Athenee Palace for old-fashioned seediness, crumbling grandeur and an air of the mysterious which at times bordered on the chilling.

The first inescapable fact about the building was the dimness of its lighting. This was oppressive at the best of times but on my arrival it appeared particularly daunting when a porter wearing a blue-peaked cap handed me from the gloom two white envelopes. Both contained telexes from London. Both – my heart sank – were addressed to Mr Bassett, *The Times* Correspondent. They were requests for copy. In the course of working for nearly three years on the paper I had received only two such missives. These had been dispatched harmlessly to a post office in Vienna. The ones I now held blew to shreds what little 'cover' I had built up in order to enter Romania. As I gazed, blinking, at the telexes I heard the porter mention my name to someone at the other end of a telephone.

From the reception to the first floor where my room was situated, a dark corridor with 15-watt bulbs at long intervals led to a black wooden spiral staircase. Every shadow seemed to hold a figure. Behind every corner I seemed to discern the unmistakable outline of the plain-clothes man I had seen at the airport. Outside my room the corridor appeared deserted but just as I turned to enter, the red glow of a cigarette end burning brightly near a sofa just twenty yards away made my flesh creep.

My bedroom window gave on to a deserted street, but I couldn't help noticing another small spot of red coming from a doorway commanding a view of my balcony. The internal decoration of the room did little to allay my fears. Opposite the bed was the largest mirror I think I have ever seen in a hotel. It took up nearly the entire height and width of the wall. In my state of mind of course it had to be a double glass. I looked at my watch, it was only 9.15 p.m., but like a child after a nightmare I longed for daylight to dispel all my anxieties and I cursed myself roundly for omitting to bring a book to distance me from my wild imaginings. I am glad to say that though I considered it, I did not barricade the door with furniture, but I don't think I have ever passed a night so utterly unprepared for sleep and so convinced that at any moment my repose would be interrupted by an uninvited guest.

In February, the sun rises late in Bucharest. Breakfast at nine could not have been any lighter than dinner at midnight. The shortage of food I had encountered on earlier visits to Romania was all too apparent. A pair of four-day-old rolls landed on my table along with a cup of murky liquid described optimistically as 'English' tea. Attempts to order any eggs or sausages only elicited a resigned shrug of the shoulders, a familiar response to any request concerning food. Even the presence of a packet of Kent cigarettes failed to improve this state of affairs though in return I received butter, jam and a small cake; this last only a day or so old.

As the sunlight filtered through the grey cloud, the view from the hotel presented itself as astonishingly attractive. To the right, outside the former royal palace, a line of soldiers tramped through the snow to change the guard. To the left rose the magnificent pile of the Athenaeum, surely one of the most picturesque concert houses in Europe. Beyond this, a large space wound its way into the middle distance. Even though much of the city was being demolished for the new boulevards of Mr Ceausescu, the Conducator as he was known here, this formal heart of the capital remained much as it had been in pre-war days. Even then, Bucharest had had to endure a passion for rebuilding on a grand scale. As Olivia Manning recounts, the square in front of the Athenee Palace was constantly littered with large pieces of cornice as King Carol erected a new edifice which might express yet more bombastically his regal pretensions. His son, like Ceausescu's son the reprobate

Nicu, also divided his spare time between fast cars and rallying the nation's youth. In this way, however bleak they appeared, affairs in Ceausescu's Romania somehow grotesquely echoed the past.

It is worth at the outset asking how a nation was capable of tolerating so much abuse and despotism. Sadly, the reason I suspect is that the very qualities which for centuries have made the Romanians some of the most affable, sensitive and chivalrous people in the Balkans have as their verso a weakness which allows evil to tread over their souls with impunity. It will be interesting indeed to see whether the post-Ceausescu era breaks the mould.

Descended, as it was always recalled in Bucharest in Ceausescu days, from the two Roman legions who occupied Dacia and who were left behind when the Empire fell, the Romanians unlike the Bulgars or Serbs are not Slavs. In their language, manners and speech, they have a far greater affinity with the Latin races of the Mediterranean than with any of their Slav neighbours. After the communist takeover this difference was exploited by the country's leaders on more than one occasion. Even Ceausescu with his eye for subtle dealing – how well he fits Metternich's phrase: 'Romania? A profession not a nation' – took advantage of this. In 1968 he condemned the Warsaw Pact invasion of Czechoslovakia. By the 1970s, he was considered by the West to be so refreshing a maverick that the Queen invited him to London. Only a few years ago Mr George Bush could amuse diplomats in Vienna on returning from Bucharest by saying that he found Romania more civilised than any other part of Eastern Europe. Since then, the repressive policies of the Ceausescu regime have become known to all. The Romanians themselves with Soviet help took the initiative at a bloody demonstration in Timisoara, in the north-west of the country, finally with army help deposing the Ceausescus who faced a suitably ignoble end by firing squad.

'The grass whose blade is not upright will not be cut by the scythe', runs an old Romanian proverb which a Bucharest friend repeated to me on our meeting later, after breakfast in the Athenee Palace. At that time it was strictly forbidden for Romanians to communicate with foreigners without informing the police within twenty-four hours. To avoid my friend getting into yet more trouble we had agreed to meet in the Amman Museum, an exquisite built by one of the country's most gifted painters, Theodor Amman.

To enter this small jewel of a building, with its faded portraits, elegant furniture and pictures of a sunny and unmistakably more bourgeois Bucharest, is to escape momentarily all the drabness communism has inflicted on the Romanians. In one corner of the drawing-room, a small oil painting shows a white-suited man in a panama hat sitting in a luxurious garden. The colouring and the brushwork suggest a hot summer in France and only the small detail of cornice with a Greek anthemion motif reveals the garden to be not in Paris but in Bucharest, in fact to be the garden of the very house which is now Amman's Museum. Gazing at such canvases it was easy to see how Bucharest had been able to call itself the Paris of the Balkans.

For a few anxious minutes I began to think my friend would not arrive or that he had misunderstood our rendezvous. As far as I could judge I had not been followed on leaving the hotel, in fact all my dark imaginings of the night before had faded with the morning sun. The museum was empty save for one old lady knitting a pullover at the door in front of a black 1900 stove. As her bulk occupied most of the portico around the stove, the temperature inside the rest of the museum was a good six degrees below zero. It seemed unlikely that there would be many visitors.

Slightly breathless but with the warmest of smiles, Mihai arrived. After a quick perusal of the *objets d'art*, including a vast canvas depicting Amman in his studio, we set off on a pedestrian tour of Bucharest. With a mixture of pride and shame at the state to which his home city had been reduced, Mihai pointed out various landmarks behind the museum as we swiftly crossed the broad avenue near the British Embassy.

We were now entering one of the few parts of the city whose street plan had not been altered by the recent demolition programme. Small winding streets of two- and three-storey houses, some in a classical style, some not, some joined to each other by peeling stucco, some separated by old plane trees, the entire ensemble in its informality certainly recalled, on a smaller scale, the picturesque nature of the Latin Quarter in Paris. Only one building, clearly dating from the post-war period, struck a discordant note. Behind the wooden panelled interior of what must have once been a well-stocked grocer's rose a cold seven-storey structure whose roof was covered by aerials and antennae. 'Not difficult to guess what that is,' Mihai said, claiming later that it was only one of eighteen secret police headquarters situated in strategic parts of each suburb.

From here, it was not very far to Mihai's house, a modest two-storey property constructed a year or two before the First World War. Inside, the walls were covered with rich carpets, Victorian wallpapers and portraits of his parents and grandparents: smartly dressed couples with bow-ties and parasols. In one corner of a darkened drawing-room there stood a few Biedermeier chairs and the odd *art nouveau* frame. The walls here were painted a dark racing green and a groaning bookshelf harboured a well-stocked library of French literature.

For the last two years my host had seen almost all of his friends starved into a state of fear in which they did not know whom they might trust. It was of course, he maintained, a deliberate ploy on the part of the authorities to ensure that everyone was so busy struggling for the essentials of life that they had no time or energy to contemplate hostile activities against the regime. Mihai did not imagine then that there would be much help coming from Gorbachev. All Moscow wanted in Romania was stability. 'After all,' he said, 'Moscow can say to everyone else in the Eastern bloc: look what happens to those countries who do not follow us.' As in Poland and elsewhere in Eastern Europe the so-called liberalisation in Moscow had not brought the communists any more respect or affection from the countries they have subjected for so long.

But by far the most distressing aspect of Romania's plight, something which the removal of the Ceausescu regime has not necessarily ended, was the erosion of old European values of trust and friendship. Everyone in Romania, one suspects even today, has a price. In order simply to eat, to find food for children and loved ones, the professional classes, doctors, university lecturers, teachers and lawyers, had difficult decisions to make. For a few packets of Kent cigarettes, the university professor was prepared to pass a failed medical student. For a week's supply of meat a doctor was prepared to perform the routine operation he would otherwise have had no time for. In such a society, Mihai insisted, only the police had the means of remaining close to their duties. They at least were well paid and had their own supplies, though this in no way inhibited their enthusiasm for corruption.

It was snowing by the time I left the house, fed on a welcome omelette, to thread my way through the streets back to the square. As so often happens, I had learnt in a few hours' conversation more about the real state of affairs in Romania than I would have learnt from the large volumes of official propaganda available in every bookshop.

In the event no official from the Foreign Ministry was waiting to pay his respects at the Athenée Palace and I slept a second night more soundly. The next morning was devoted to examining building projects of the Ceausescus in the city centre. Access to these was to be given by a young architect who had actually been forced to work on the designs for the mad Conducator. Barely in his thirties and with a shrewd command of English and French he possessed in abundance that quality of all Romanians who have preserved their sanity, an excellent sense of humour. As far as could be seen, he enjoyed few privileges for being engaged on work of such prestigious character. In return for overseeing a quarter of a mile of one of the many interminable boulevards, he was allowed access neither to special food supplies nor to government petrol stations. He had walked to work past a queue of three hundred vehicles abandoned outside a public petrol station for the last four weeks.

Style apparently was the most crucial issue for his patron. But here the Conducator was overruled by his wife, the domineering Elena whose influence was so formidable that on at least two occasions entire buildings recently constructed had to be, within days, demolished and re-erected in a new style. On another occasion, she had attempted to understand some drawings sent to her for approval. The chief architect spent twenty-five minutes explaining the details of the lavish bathroom facilities before the commanding voice interrupted with the words, 'Build a model. I would like a model.' 'Certainly,' replied the architect, and later he presented an immaculate vision in miniature of his creation. Unfortunately the model was too small for Elena who insisted on nothing less than a 1:1 scale model which took six months to construct. As this did not meet with her approval that part of the boulevard had to be demolished yet again. Mrs Ceausescu's whims had set back the entire project by months. Nor were these the only trials. Like

Sansovino working for the Venetian doges, the court architects ran the risk of incarceration should their buildings fail to meet expectations.

In their half-completed form the long boulevards carved out of the once rambling townscape of Bucharest appeared like a nightmarish fantasy – hollow concrete shells stretching as far as the eye could see. Even without the enormous ditches and mud holes surrounding them, it was difficult to imagine that they could ever afford more agreeable housing than that which was destroyed to make way for them.

Around Constitution Square the megalomaniac constructions of an earlier era rose like a scene out of Fritz Lang's *Metropolis*. A skyscraper in the Stalinist vocabulary familiar in Warsaw and Moscow presented a particularly sinister residence for the 'Ministry of Information'. Perhaps because the fog had closed in, as it does so frequently in Bucharest in the winter, these buildings whose top storeys were lost in the grey sky appeared doubly unreal.

Mihai was keen to take me to a restaurant where he assured me there would be something to eat as it was occasionally visited by Party people. Situated in a barn of a building in a distant suburb, despite the three-page menu there seemed to be precious little available. We all sat in our coats. Our breath could be seen for almost six seconds after we exhaled. Ironically the only dish freely available was ice-cream. Despite the bleak temperature this unsuitable fare was seized on with relish by a couple of visiting foreign ministry officials.

In the afternoon, to escape all this greyness, we drove – after an Odyssian search for petrol – to Mogosoaia, a small park with a pretty palace in the Romanian feudal style a few miles east of Bucharest. The drive illustrated the extraordinary flatness of Bucharest's surroundings. Like Warsaw, the Stalinist blocks of Bucharest dominate the landscape for miles, rising up like sinister castles in the air. With relief the remains of the old Mogosoaia palace brought us rapidly into a more gentle world. Here in the woods close to the palace there were faint echoes of a lost chivalry. Overgrown tombs, whose crumbling scripts told of 'heroic exploits' in a cavalry skirmish, reminded the visitor of nobler days.

Mihai in a most understated way was something of a nationalist. These remains meant as much to him as the crown jewels I had seen in Budapest meant to the Hungarians. Such was Mihai's pride that though I never heard him once say a negative word about the Hungarians who so violently despised the Romanians, he refused to accept a fine Hungarian salami which I brought for him from an expensive delicatessen in Budapest.

Mihai pointed out how much of the palace was falling to bits uninhibited either by officials or funds. The contents of the palace had long been sacked by the communists but what little original fabric remained was now in danger of disappearing entirely over the next few months. In the crisp, cold air there was a haunting melancholy about the place. Nowhere else in the Balkans was the inevitable comparison between present and past so depressing. In Bucharest the contrast is painful enough even to those who never knew the city before the war. But perhaps material deprivation, mental oppression and moral collapse have been part of the human condition in this part of the world for so long that life continues nevertheless with a quiet dignity.

That evening I went to the Athenaeum to hear the orchestra play Brahms. The performance was not outstanding though it was very musical – the Romanian strings in particular warming to the Fourth Symphony's romantic opening. What made the evening memorable was the audience. Dressed in the tired suits and dresses which were common in the 1950s, they listened rapt throughout. Their gestures, if they made any gestures, were singular and elegant. For them the Brahms was not just a musical diversion but a brief deeply treasured period of escape allowing the mind to wander free in another world. During the interval they had gathered in small groups of threes and fours in the unlit and unheated Athenaeum foyer whose 'crush bar', no doubt once elegant, was permanently closed. Few people smiled though brave faces could be seen grimly watching each other's breath, silently gazing at the architecture. At the end there were no cars or buses to take the audience home. In three inches of snow, people trudged back to unlit and unheated rooms to eat some soup and drink some home-distilled spirit. Their very presence at the concert spoke eloquently of Ceausescu's failure to crush the innate civilised spirit of the Romanian people.

As in North-Eastern Europe the collapse of communism in the Balkans is almost complete. New arrangements will have to be made after the artificial order of tyranny which has reigned over most of Central and South-Eastern Europe disappears. The Balkans being the Balkans, however, it is highly unlikely that this long overdue transition can be accomplished peacefully. That is only fair perhaps. Those who have ruined the lives of millions may not deserve to be allowed to retire without some act of expiation. If they do, it will be a tribute to the civilisation of the late twentieth century. In Jugoslavia, crowds manipulated by unscrupulous politicians gather to demand arms. In Romania a popular revolt has sealed in blood the fate of a system which ruled with a combination of feudal deprivation and modern terror. As the peninsula approaches the twenty-first century one can only echo Sir Arthur Bullivant's oft-quoted words to Richard Hannay in *Greenmantle*: 'There is a dry wind blowing in the east. The parched grasses await the spark.'

SELECT BIBLIOGRAPHY

Armstrong, Hamilton Fish, *Where the East Begins*, New York, 1929.

Baedeker, *Austria Hungary*, tenth edition, Leipzig, 1905.

Baker, J., *Austria: Her People and Her Lands*, London, 1908.

Barry, Lt.-Col. P., *The Gates of the East*, London, 1906.

Brooke Shepherd, Gordon, *Tragedy at Sarajevo*, London 1985.

Casson, Stanley, *Some Modern Sculptors*, London, 1928.

Etherton, Lt.-Col., *Through Europe and the Balkans*, London, 1928.

Gedye, G. E. R., *Heirs to the Habsburgs*, Bristol, 1932.

Gordon, Jan and Cora, *Two Vagabonds in the Balkans*, London, 1925.

Grogan, Lady, *Life of J. D. Bourchier*, London, 1922.

Hamilton, Lord F., *The Vanished Pomps of Yesterday*, London, 1921.

Herbert, Aubrey, *Ben Kendim*, London, 1924.

Jackson, F. Hamilton, *The Shores of the Adriatic*, London, 1908.

Lehmann, John, *Down River*, London, 1938.

Lyall, Archibald, *The Balkan Road*, London, 1930.

Mitton, G., *Austria Hungary*, London, 1915.

Newman, Bernard, *The Blue Danube*, London, 1929.

Powell, N., *Travellers to Trieste*, London, 1978.

Stamer, W., *Continental Road Travel*, London, 1906.

Wandruska, A., *The House of Habsburg*, London, 1964.

INDEX

141